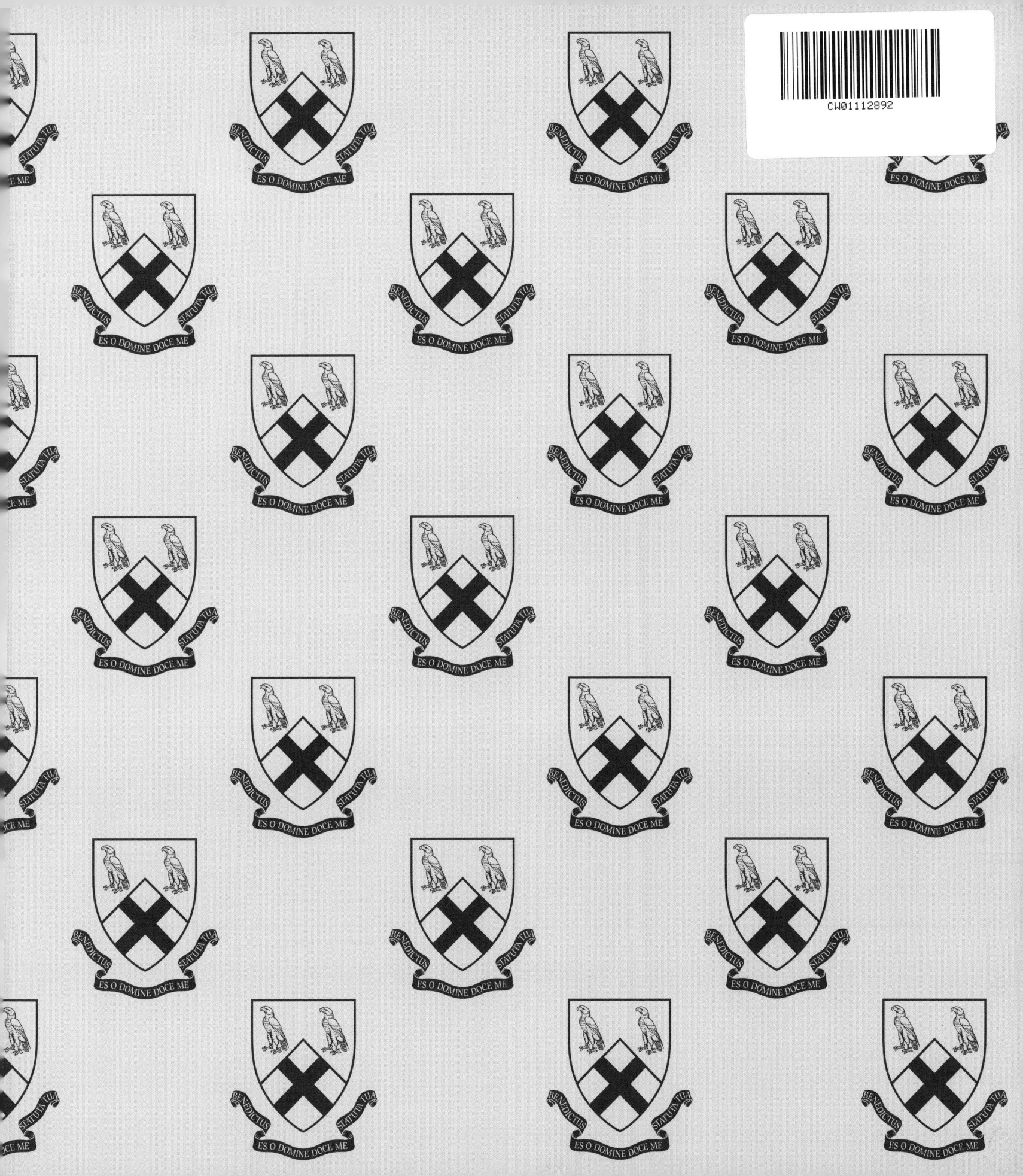

# BRADFIELD 175

*A Celebration of Bradfield's 175-year history*

# BRADFIELD COLLEGE

1850 **175** 2025

# BRADFIELD 175

*A Celebration of Bradfield's 175-year history*

UNICORN

# CONTENTS

| | |
|---|---|
| FOREWORD | 6 |
| SEPTEMBER | 10 |
| OCTOBER | 44 |
| NOVEMBER | 58 |
| DECEMBER | 92 |
| JANUARY | 100 |
| FEBRUARY | 124 |
| MARCH | 136 |
| APRIL | 160 |
| MAY | 168 |
| JUNE | 188 |
| JULY | 210 |
| THE GREEK PLAY | 224 |
| AUGUST | 248 |
| ST ANDREW'S | 258 |
| AFTERWORD | 270 |

# FOREWORD

Saint Andrew's College, Bradfield, was founded by the Reverend Thomas Stevens in 1850 with a view to the long term. He oversaw the establishment of a distinctive campus in harmony with its beautiful rural setting, making use of local materials and local craftsmen. Whilst hinting at the severe financial difficulties he encountered, the Founder's prayer speaks of the manner in which his educational project and his vision have ultimately flourished.

This anniversary volume testifies to the natural rhythms of the Pang Valley and the academic year. Its images witness the changing of seasons and the changing of society but also demonstrate that enduring power of the place and of the people fortunate to know it. Like the many trees that are a feature of our campus, Bradfield has grown, spread its branches and changed subtly each year, but so much pupil activity remains instantly recognisable.

Revd Thomas Stevens, the Founder, in 1879.

The story of the College told through these pages emerges as social history, portraying in microcosm a world that becomes more diverse, more open, and more outward looking, and that sees girls and women take their rightful place. Meanwhile, the pleasures of human interaction, learning new wonders and mastering new skills appear reassuringly enduring and unchanging.

Thomas Stevens would have been saddened to see his parish Church fall into disuse, but he would be consoled and perhaps excited to see it take its place at the heart of Bradfield's campus and education some 175 years later. In many ways, its story of regeneration is symbolic of the College's history. As Tancredi says to his world-weary uncle in Lampedusa's *The Leopard*, which traces society's rapid changes as it emerges from the nineteenth century, 'sometimes everything has to change in order for everything to stay the same.'

**Dr Christopher Stevens, Headmaster**

'The same William [son of Ansculf] holds Bradfield. Horling held it of King Edward. It was then assessed at 9 hides; now at 6 hides. There is land for 30 ploughs. In demesne are 2 ploughs; and 20 villeins and 31 bordars with 18 ploughs. There are 9 slaves, and 3 mills rendering 53s, and 20 acres of meadow, woodland for 100 pigs. Then, and afterwards, it was worth 241; now 161. The same William holds for 30 ploughs. In demesne are 2 ploughs, 20 villeins and 31 bordars with 18 ploughs. There are 9 slaves, and 3 mills rendering 53 shillings, and 20 acres of meadow. Woodland at 100 pigs. In the time of King Edward, and afterwards, it was worth £24; now £16.'

Bradefelt's entry in the Domesday Book, 1086.

Bradfield has been farmed for over 2,000 years. The valley is scattered with prehistoric remains, and Bradfield's origins predate even the Roman villa that once sat at its northern edge. After the Romans, Bradfield served as a Saxon minster: the ruler of Wessex, King Ina, granted the land ('Bradenfeld') to Eadfrith, who founded the minster in ad 670. Significantly, this is one of the earliest minsters in Berkshire, which had only recently been Christianised.

Under the Saxons, Bradfield played a role in King Alfred's triumphs. Indeed, the first recorded English victory against the Danes is the Battle of Englefield (871) where the Vikings were defeated by a hastily assembled volunteer army from Bradfield and the surrounding villages. Alfred himself fought at that battle.

A map of the village from 1382. Several features still form the College today: see the apocryphal 'monastery' wall that is thought to be the remnants of a grand medieval hall; the Tom O'Bedlam Hole named after the pariah who ostensibly lived in it; the forge which has received so many commissions from the College. But note also the repositioning of the main gate and the ubiquity of stately and agricultural buildings. The Hogger path is now referred to as 'Hog's Back Path', and the chalk pit has become the Greek Theatre.

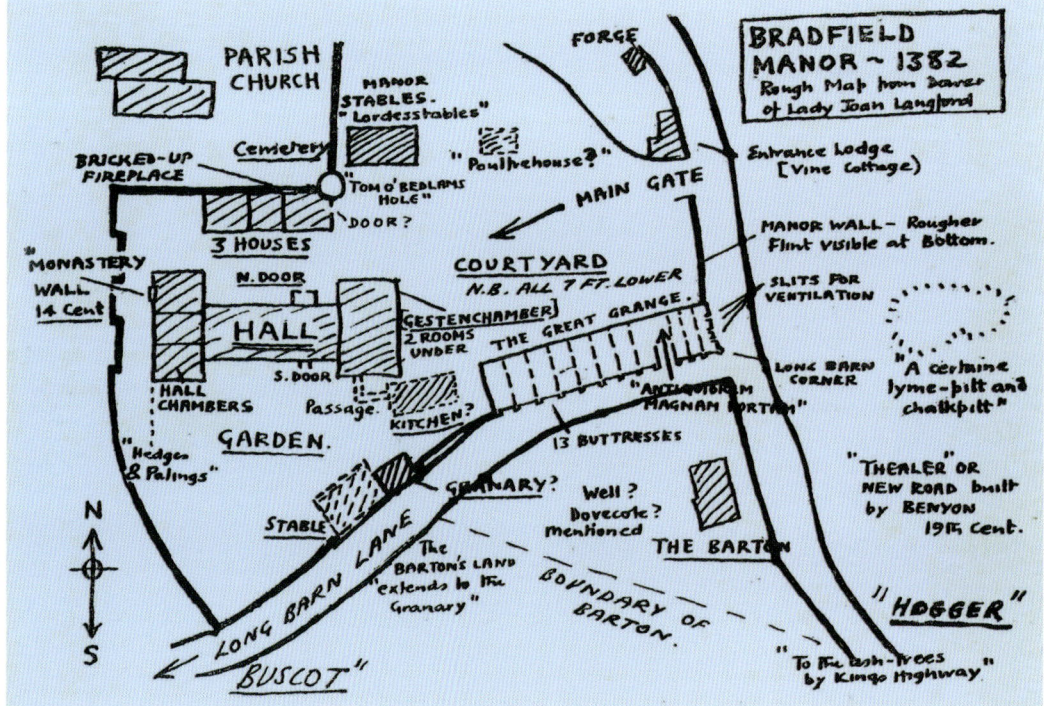

Bradfield in 2025. The confluence of 1382 is now the crossroads.

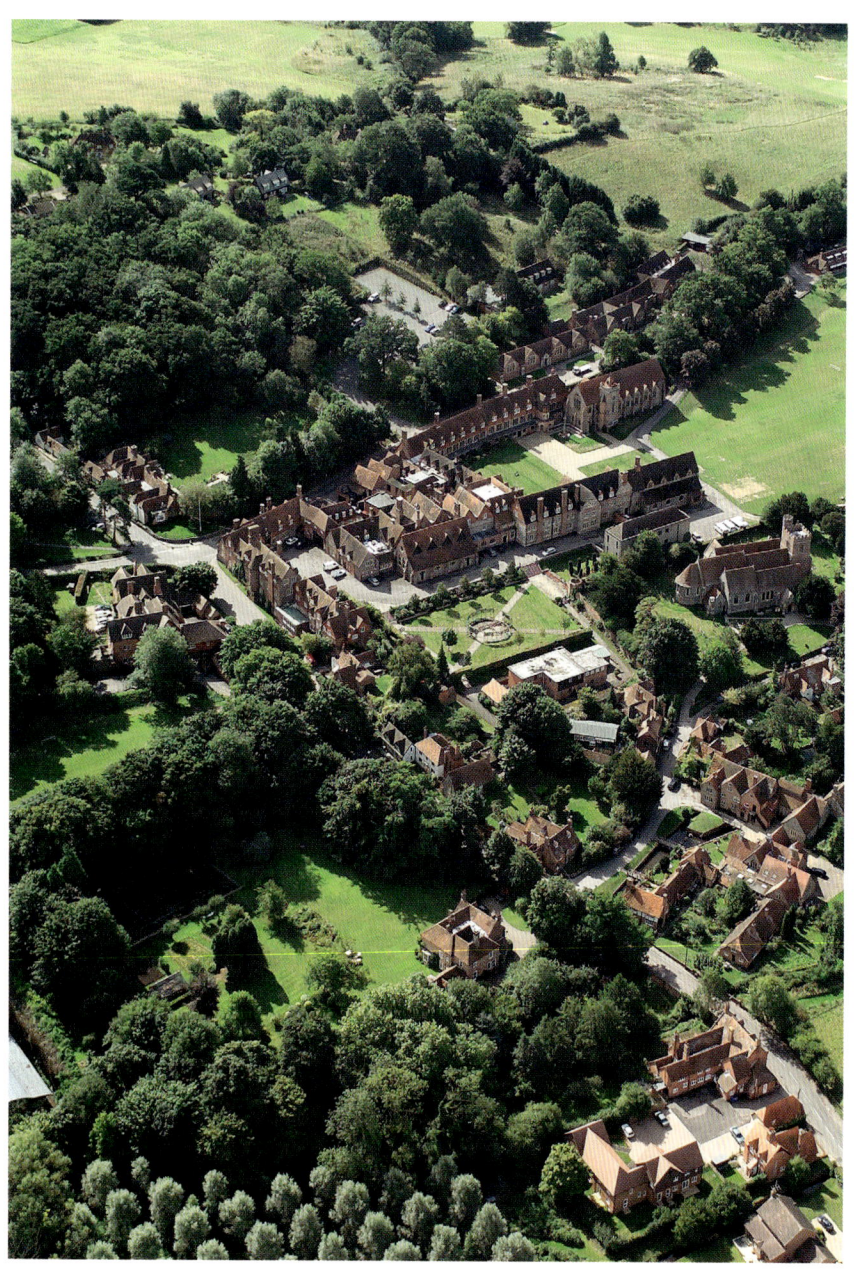

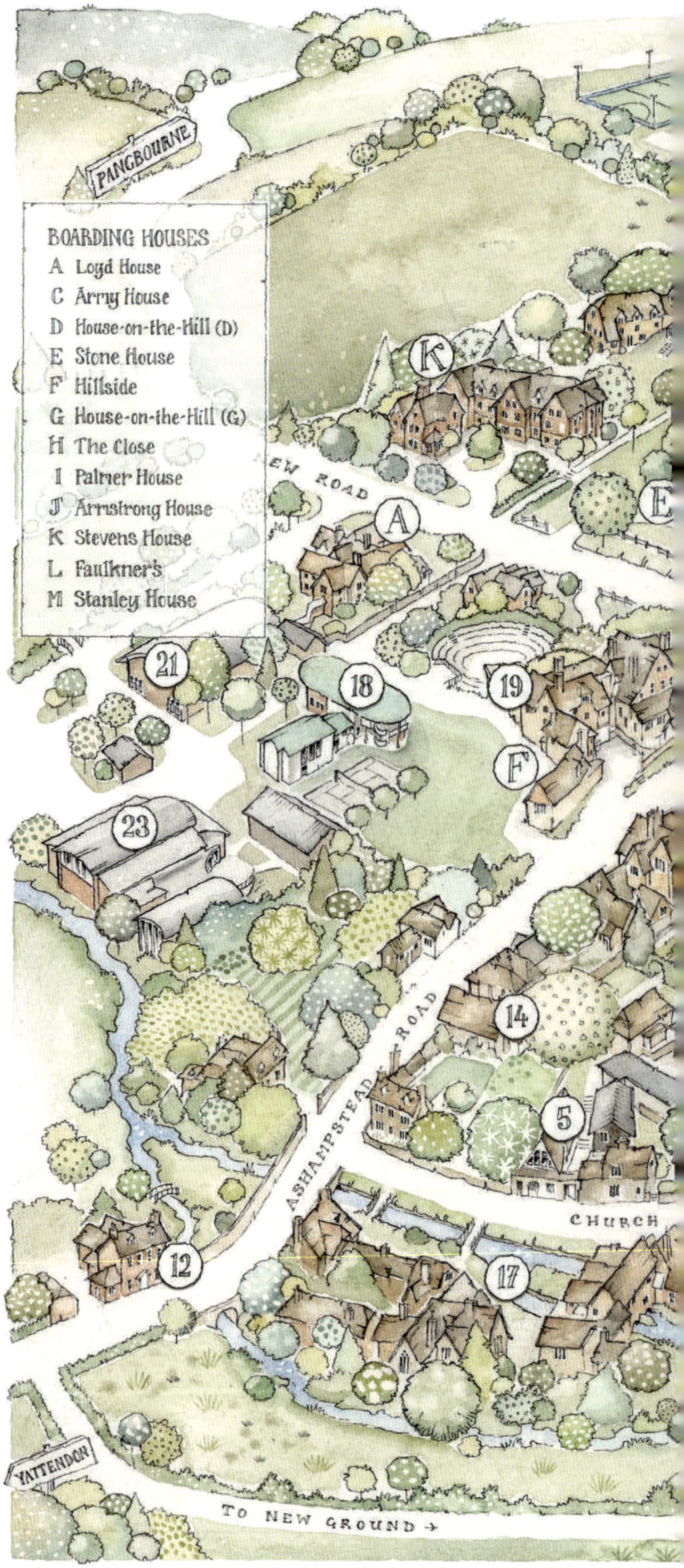
PANGBOURNE
BOARDING HOUSES
A Loyd House
C Army House
D House-on-the-Hill (D)
E Stone House
F Hillside
G House-on-the-Hill (G)
H The Close
I Palmer House
J Armstrong House
K Stevens House
L Faulkner's
M Stanley House
NEW ROAD
ASHAMPSTEAD ROAD
CHURCH
YATTENDON
TO NEW GROUND →

# SEPTEMBER

## NEW BEGINNINGS

Whilst September brings the return of many to the valley, it signals the beginning for a very special group of fresh-faced Faulkner's pupils as they step outside of their small ponds into what undoubtedly feels like the ocean. Although a little unsure, they are quickly swept up in the warm currents created by the various tutors, matrons, teachers, and coaches who stand beside them as they learn what it means to be part of a community, navigating the highs and lows as they strive for excellence, and all the while forging lifelong friendships in the process. The key message to the pupils is to 'work hard, be kind, and get involved', and as their confidence grows and they learn to be the best version of themselves, we count ourselves lucky to help them thrive and flourish in everything that they do. I can only hope that the young men and women streaming through the Faulkner's doors are starting a journey that is as enjoyable as the one I began over 20 years ago just over the Green in G House and I feel incredibly honoured and proud to have the opportunity to do what I can to help them thrive in this very special school.

**Mr J. Fox, OB and Housemaster of Faulkner's Boys**

Although the school was founded in 1850 with the modest ambition of filling the parish choir stalls, students now come from around the world for a Bradfield education. Whether disembarking from a horse-drawn stagecoach or alighting at Heathrow, pupils have always known an escape from the humdrum of the urban and the frenetic. Bradfield's charm is instantly known in its fields, its rivers, and its birdsong.

And so the new year begins with the return to Bradfield. The scene in the early 1900s may have been more verdant, but the sylvan charm has never been lost.

In 2025, the arrival is no less evocative. Anvils may now be stilled and horses automotive, but the great trees of Bradfield still stand in welcome.

The familiar approach. Crossing the Pang, the greeting clang of the anvil would carry you up your final hill. The forge on the right fashioned much of the ironwork around the College, including the gates beneath the archway. Indeed, there has been a forge on that site for over 700 years. On the left, just out of shot, is Bradfield's Roman Catholic Chapel, built to make accommodation for Roman Catholic worship.

In 2025, the arrival is no less evocative. Anvils may now be stilled and horses automotive, but the great trees of Bradfield still stand in welcome.

The aforementioned old Roman Catholic Chapel behind the foliage. Its use spent, it then became a barber's shop and then a drum rehearsal room.

SEPTEMBER

Or perhaps, upon one's return, you choose to circle up past St Andrew's Church, so vital to the College's ontology. The café was incorporated into the College as the Second Master's house, but is now in private ownership. To its right, the old post office is now the College sculpture studio and Photography department. The running stream beneath the mill still sounds alongside an unchanging view with perfect harmony. The College bought the entire mill in 1920.

Facing the mill, the College Art department, built in 1862. Originally, it was the local village primary school.

Girls from that primary school pose above the mill-stream.

SEPTEMBER

After a steady climb or keen descent, one reaches the crossroads. These views have hardly altered over the past century. Army House still crowns the slope, and its turrets give one's arrival a momentous but familiar grandeur.

For 156 years, the College archway has served as its main entrance, and witnesses the flow of a thousand staff and students daily.

The oldest part of the College sits inconspicuously in the bottom right. The buttress is that of the medieval tithe barn (see map at opening) that has since evolved into the present incarnation.

The rooms above the archway now belong to the boys of Army House (C), but historically it was the writing room of the Founder. Thomas Stevens was supremely well connected, and great men and women of the age were written to from that room. Many of those letters now reside in the College archive.

The treasured view as one enters the College has ever been consistent, with the sweeping fields rolling up to Greathouse Wood.

And today, even in the haste of all their commitments, students can still raise their eyes to the slopes of the valley.

SEPTEMBER

In times gone by, as now, the old lodge warded the entrance to the estate. In this photograph, the sloping and towered arm of Army House (C) is yet to be built, and the archway will not be raised until 1866.

The section atop the lodge was called the Continent Room, or a 'san' as we might know it today. It was designed on the advice of Florence Nightingale, whose experiences in the Crimean War proved invaluable. Her rather scathing letter to the College is pictured here.

The Continent Room had been constructed by 1865 in response to an outbreak of scarlet fever which had gripped the nation in 1863. It was so-called because the boys who were sent there were 'incontinent', from the Latin 'not holding together'; ill, in other words.

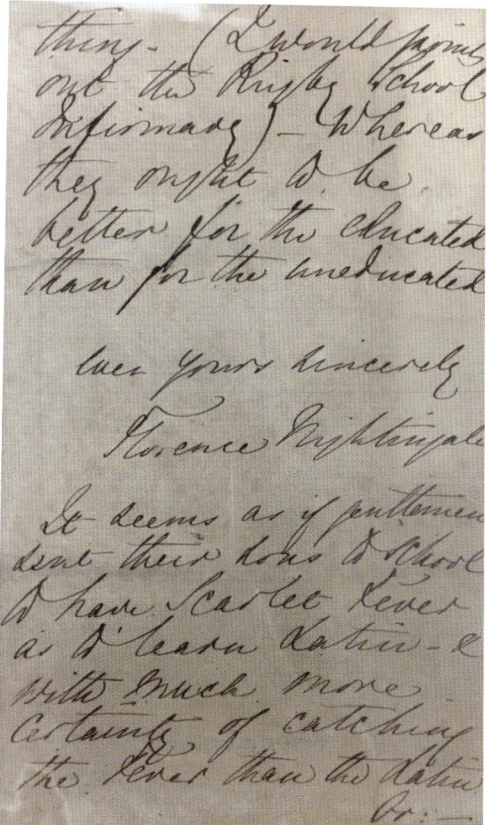

By 1882, the College has its first boarders, although the term 'house' was not used. Rather, they were housed in 'Army Side', so named because of the predestined profession of its occupants. In fact, for many years the houses followed entirely different curriculums from one another: classical for some, naval for another, and land warfare for these, and so on. Thus, you would be educated with your house, and not with the wider school. Here stands Army Side in 1906.

SEPTEMBER

Circling round the corner, the beauty of the campus is all the more evident. The Thai Garden creates an oasis in our busy midst, and the flinty flank of the Quad serves as an expression of Bradfield's unique identity and architecture. To the right, the Scholar's Garden, laid out in 1930.

The Thai Garden is an ideal place to learn, meet, or lunch.

SEPTEMBER

Remarkably, this too has changed little. The Headmaster's Lawn, once a tennis court, is now the Thai Garden. It was converted by the OB Thai Community in thanks from the students of Thailand; it also serves as a reminder of Bradfield's international reach and community, something the Founder could not have foreseen in 1850. The buildings are much the same, but note the vents atop the Dining Hall (below).

These mysterious doors are believed to lead to cellars below the dining hall.

Here, the Headmaster's Lawn is pictured in 1906. For many years it was a key site in the 'Bumph Test', a trial for new boys, who were asked the names of the three trees on the lawn. The correct answer was 'Tom, Dick and Harry, but Harry died'. Failure resulted in a hasty jog to the next village, Bradfield Southend, where the war memorial was to be studied for further questioning.

SEPTEMBER

Of course, the Quad is and has always been the heart of the College. Walking back onto the green in September doubtless reminds us all of the beauty and endeavour of where we learn and work.

For many years, the Quad was the site of the handshaking tradition. Masters would span the Quad in almost complete darkness and await the emergence of the boys from the gloom. Inevitably, many boys saw fit to go round several times and thus prolong the evening indefinitely.

However, the Quad is not such by initial design, but by steady addition. Here it is in 1864: the manor house has been extended to the right to eventually accommodate boarding (A House). The manor house itself (below) was built in 1837. Big School is yet to be added, as is Bloods and the chapel.

Bradfield Place in 1845. There has been a manor house on this site since before the Middle Ages.

And here is the north side of Quad in 1874, two years after Big School was added. The gabled connection back to the manor house was added in 1869.

**And since then, naught has changed!**

SEPTEMBER

But what of the south side? If one looks closely at the photograph in the top left, one can see that the south side of Quad is yet to be built. Budgeons Yard is behind, so called due to the servants that were made available to the boys and staff.

It was not until 1897 that the south side of the Quad was completed, although the extensions began in the 1880s. Called Bloods Corridor, a Blood was a prefect (often chosen due to sporting prowess) and this salient of the Quad was their domain. In the absence of housemasters, who lived separately, and predating common rooms, the boys spent their evenings socialising in the classrooms ('form rooms') and the Bloods held sway.

Note the tennis courts on the green, an act that would cause more than a little consternation today.

The groundwork for the chapel was laid in 1892, and it was originally smaller. It would be completed by 1903, photographed here in 1906 *sans* the tower, which will rise in 1914.

Indeed, the College has had many faces over the years. Once a grand manor house, several of its contemporary corners still hearken back to those times. However, the College entrance looks unrecognisable here.

As does the Headmaster's Corridor, then a museum and now the Senior Common Room. These halls are since bereft of their weaponry, rendering the Quad largely defenceless.

SEPTEMBER

Comfortingly, the Dining Hall, built in 1856, is a true constant. The hall is still weighted with history: the windows were stained by the great pre-Raphaelite artist Sir Edward Burne-Jones, and Oxbridge scholars from days gone by have their names hammered onto gold plates in the pillars. Indeed, several members of the College Council also have their names on such plates, including four-time prime minister William Gladstone. The 10 pillars that lift the hall are all the shaped trunks of elm trees.

Despite the tenure of the surroundings, the ceremony has changed somewhat. The High Table was the preserve of the masters until the 1970s, but has since been removed. Until recently, the boys sat in houses, and each meal was concluded by four pupils singing a Latin grace.

What is more, for much of the hall's life, the masters and students had been served upon by waiters known as budgeons, meaning 'servants', who wore blue coats with brass buttons.

In the 19th century, the boys generally ate their daily meals with beer brewed at the Rectory.

Light shines through the Burne-Jones windows. Below, a Greek inscription by Headmaster Gray – 'Hard work overcomes a lazy disposition' – serves as a warning against indolence. Aesop's *Hare and Tortoise* fable is pictured above, as if to ensure the warning is heeded even by those who cannot be bothered with the inscription.

William Morris assisted with these windows, which depict the expulsion from Eden, the tumult of Babel, and the pomp of the Queen of Sheba.

The College grace, still read in the Latin before formal meals, hangs by the door.

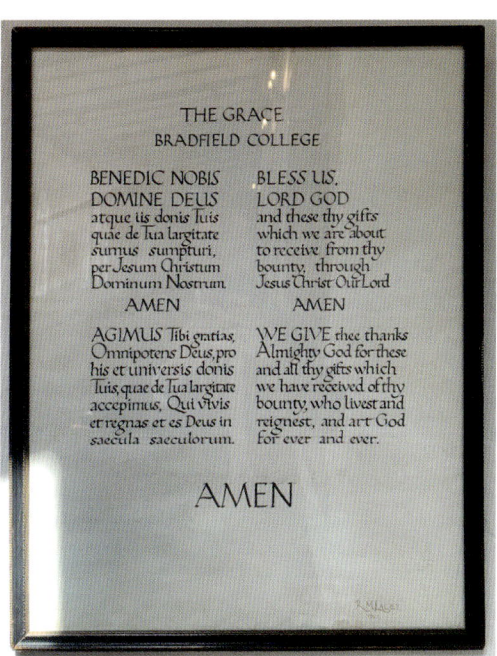

SEPTEMBER

And so the College thus surveyed stands in welcome.

Faulkner's are amongst the first to arrive, full of daunt and thrill. And though the modern drop-off is a rather more familial affair than times gone by, some things never change. Note the boarders' chests, the autumn glow, and the start-of-term hum. Many are boarding for the first time.

SEPTEMBER

There is no question that the formality of schooling has lessened over the years. Gone are the gowns and mortars, replaced by a less austere September. Here, the boys of 1893 likewise begin their year.

The housemaster ensures a warm welcome.

SEPTEMBER

Seeing the arrival of Faulkner's puts one in mind of the very first arrival, namely Blackall Simonds, who was initially educated alone until more boys were recruited. He arrived in the February, then Richard Binfield in the March, and then three more boys in August.

His brother, George, was an eminent sculptor, creating the war memorial in the Quad.

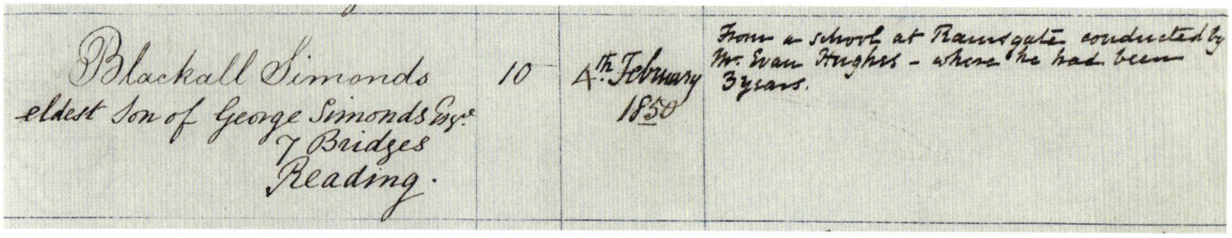
Blackall Simonds
eldest Son of George Simonds Esqr
7 Bridges
Reading.
10
4th February
1850
From a school at Ramsgate conducted by Mr Evan Hughes - where he had been 3 years.

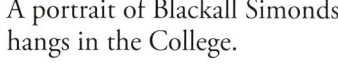

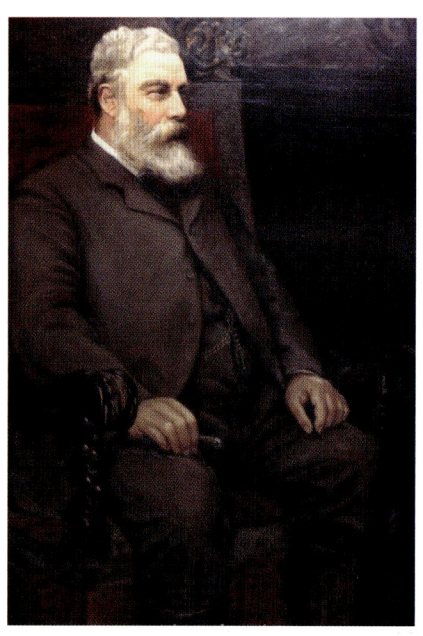

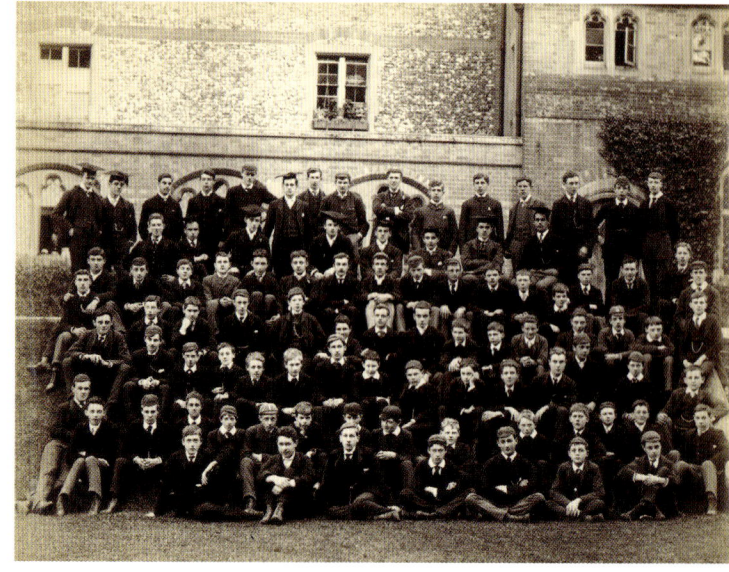

A portrait of Blackall Simonds hangs in the College.

The whole school in 1885.

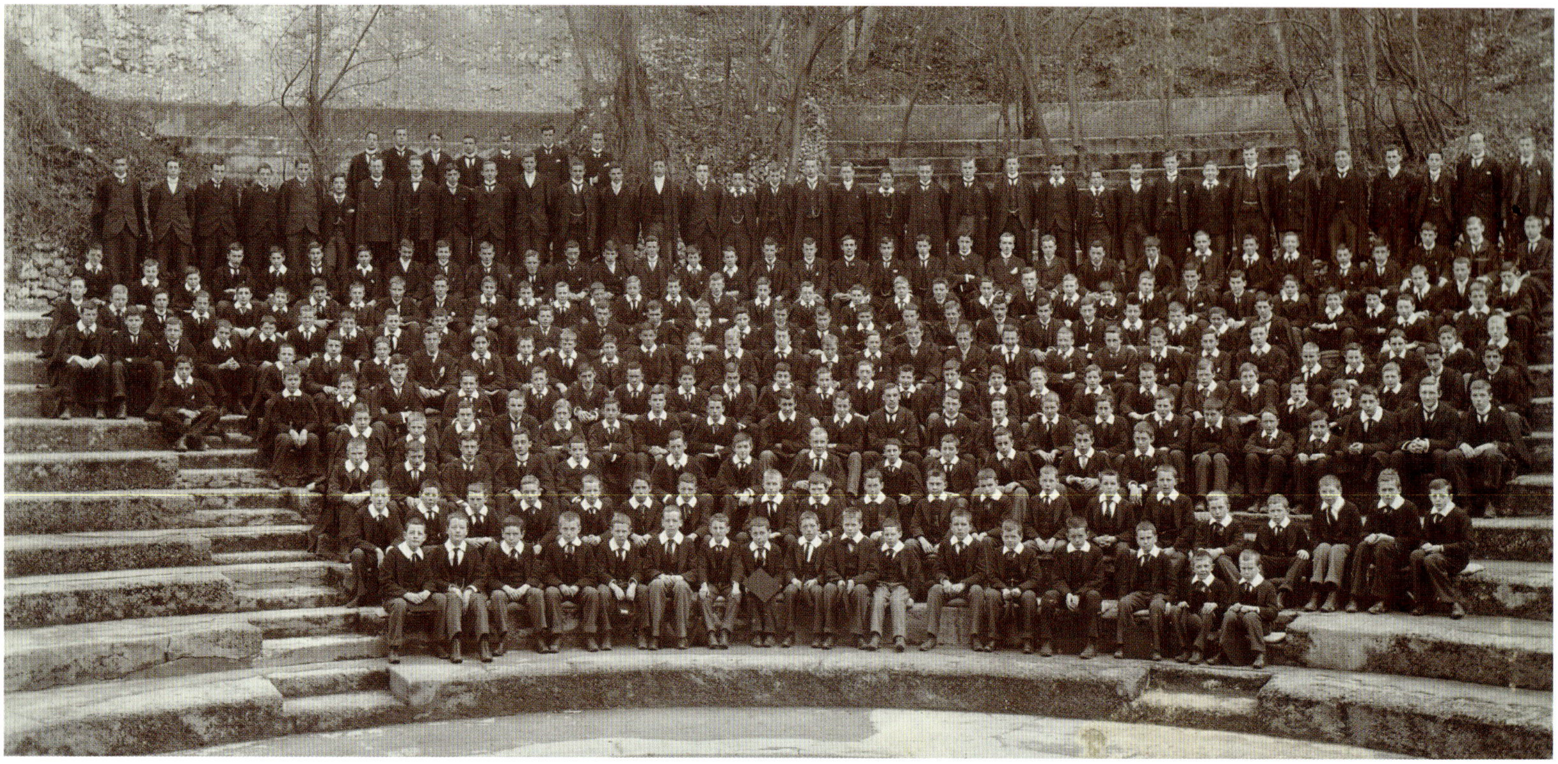

By 1900, the numbers in September had increased significantly.

Upon arrival, perhaps the first thing to get to grips with is Bradfield's strange language. This 1999 guide helps newcomers (then called the 4th Form) navigate from Snaker through Jellies so that they are not late for their ruxing.

**NEW PUPILS' GUIDE 1999**

## BRADFIELD 'SPEAK'.

As with many schools, Bradfield has its own vocabulary which has been built up over the course of the last 150 years. It is probably not as extensive as some but nevertheless, there are some important words that you should be familiar with. Here is a list of those currently in use:

**Cheesing** — Doing cross country. This may be one of the first bits of Bradfield slang that you come across as the Fourth Form Cheese is usually very near to the start of term.

**Ruxing** — A rux is a practice in any sport but it is usually applied to football hockey and cricket. Each house has an area which they can call their ruxing ground. The best area is probably the Hillside ruxing ground.

**Snaker** — Snaker is the main door to the school - 'Snake Door'.

**Jellies (Passage)** — The corridor leading from the main school dining hall. It is an area full of notice boards, games, CCF, D of E etc.

**Bloods (Passage)** — The ground floor corridor in the main part of school leading to the chapel.

**Greeker** — The Greek Theatre.

**The San** — The San is the school hospital and is found by going down the hill from Faulkner's, going straight over at the crossroads and The San is the first building on your right after you cross the River Pang.

**SCR** — Senior Common Room - Where most teachers go for some peace and quiet and a cup of coffee during break. It is located opposite Gray Schools, the modern languages building.

**JCR** — The JCR is the name given to the body of school prefects in the Upper Sixth.

**Brewer** — The name given to the cooking areas in the pupils houses.

**Beaks / Cops** — Prefects.

**Woo** — This is being in a bad mood. Hopefully this won't apply to you very often!

**Old Greek Street** — Old Greek Street is the name of the path which runs from behind the Science departments up the hill. It is also known by a rather less pleasant name.

SEPTEMBER

Settled in, it is not long before the formalities, rigours, and traditions of term begin to sound their unique rhythm. The Handshaking Service is one of Bradfield's foremost traditions, where each student shakes the hand of each master and mistress. Dr Stevens, the current headmaster, is seen below.

SEPTEMBER

Nor are the houses idle. September brings a number of house events to the fore, not least house debating, fought with great passion no matter the motion. Here, students of all ages can demonstrate their wit, zeal, and guile.

The Debating Society at Bradfield is formidable and traces its history back to 1854.

SEPTEMBER

SEPTEMBER

SEPTEMBER

However, September's crowning glory is Goose, where the College turns all matters over to a relentless and thrilling weekend of fiercely fought competitions. For a 'closed weekend', every conceivable sport and activity converge within the village, and all are worth vital points towards the coveted Goose Trophy. Current wisdom is that CCF boots are the key to a tug-of-war victory.

Goose is so named due to its proximity in the calendar to the Michaelmas Goose Fair. A marble goose is the spoil for the victors. It was once mistakenly decapitated by a head of English, but has subsequently been restored.

Goose is the perfect way to integrate the new 'Shell' into their senior houses. They readily serve their new allegiance, often calculating that many hours spent at certain activities reaps the most points for the house!

SEPTEMBER

All this culminates on the final night with House Song, a rigorously rehearsed and strictly choreographed fest of musical renditions. Held in Greeker, the chants reverberate around the cauldron until tradition takes over and perfect silence is observed. In many ways, the evening is the best of Bradfield: a night of pure spirit steeped in legacy.

SEPTEMBER

As a final touch, the Faulkner's, still so new to the College, are invited to perform what they have prepared. As is customary, each of the senior students holds a light aloft and the final applause is uproarious.

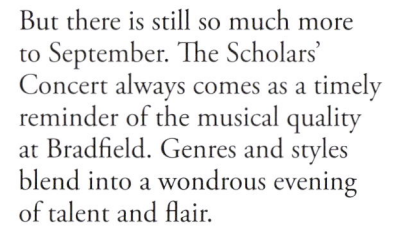

But there is still so much more to September. The Scholars' Concert always comes as a timely reminder of the musical quality at Bradfield. Genres and styles blend into a wondrous evening of talent and flair.

SEPTEMBER

And despite the year being so young, elite sport waits for no one. Here, our 1st XI girls play Bedford in the Hockey National Cup…

… and our 1st XI girls tussle with Brentwood in the ISFA Cup.

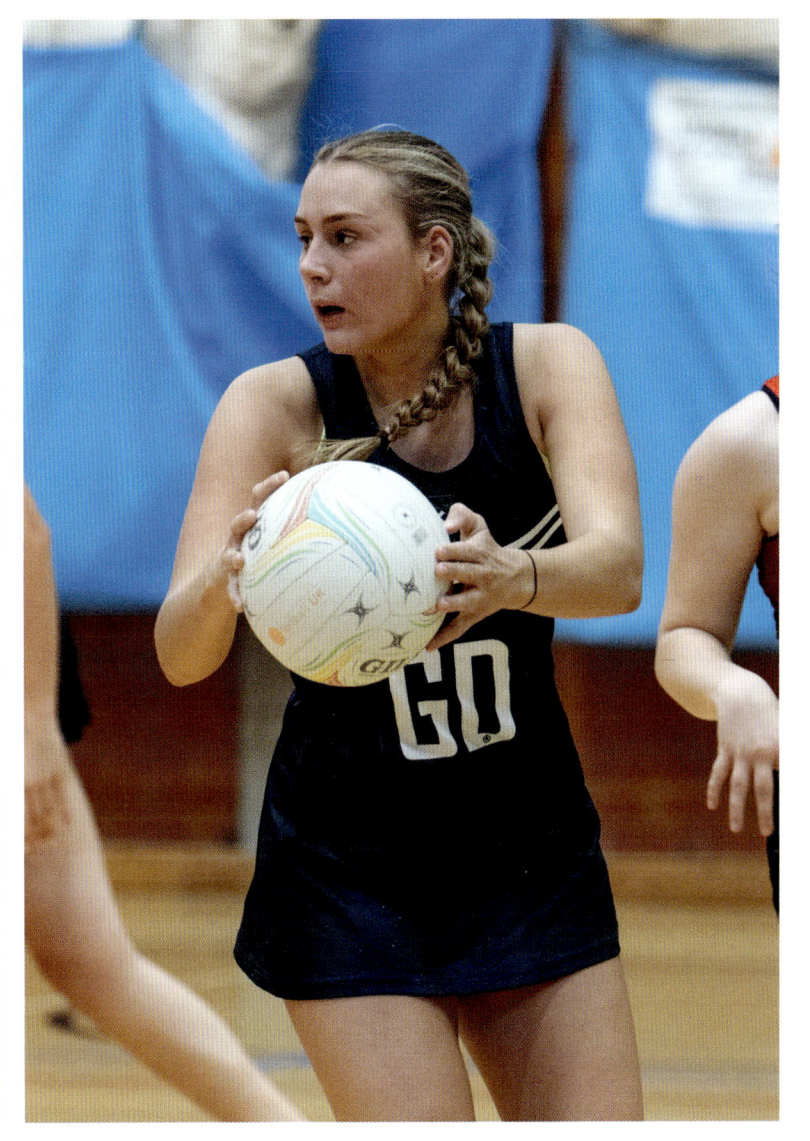

… and our 1st VII prevail over King's Worcester in the Netball National Cup.

SEPTEMBER

# OCTOBER

## TEACHING AND LEARNING

In the brisk, invigorating air of October, Bradfield College awakens with the spirit of discovery and growth. As the summer fades, the freshly pressed uniforms and pristine books of Michaelmas term start to show the marks of enthusiastic use. Pupils of Faulkner's stand taller, embracing the challenges of an interconnected curriculum with a sense of adventure. Shell pupils and the Lower Sixth flourish in their chosen subjects, with the latter beginning to navigate the higher expectations and newfound independence of their studies.

The Upper Sixth, now leading the school, bring an invigorated approach to their learning as they contemplate the next steps for life after Bradfield. Their leadership and dedication inspire the entire school community.

Bradfield's vision for learning is not static; it is a dynamic journey that evolves with each passing day. The aim is to bestow upon students the gifts of critical thinking, resilience, and an enduring passion for knowledge: an education for life. In this vibrant season, the thrill of learning is ever-present, making October a pivotal time for intellectual and personal development at Bradfield College.

**Mrs E. Wells, Director of Studies**

The College's ethos instilled in me a determination and motivation to make my dreams a reality in both my career and personal life.

**Hattie Pearson (K-08), Hits Radio Presenter and DJ**

Alongside all the co-curricular excitement of the start of the year, the College does not forget its primary focus: the teaching and learning of its young people. Observing these students of the past, one can be forgiven for seeing a distance between our and their school experience. We are drawn to these distinctions, but the horseplay of the boys on Pit reminds us that these are, after all, teenagers, eager and ready to learn about the world that they shall soon inherit. What is more, that photo was taken in 1917, a time when the sombre cliché would be well excused.

Gowns will not be abolished until 2001.

OCTOBER

Even if teenagers have stayed broadly the same, the spaces where they learn have evolved. At the turn of the last century, classrooms would appear regimented to the modern eye: rows facing forwards with the emphasis not on a fronted display, but on one's own desk. Here in Big School, a painting of the Founder looms above them.

Atop Big School is the Beaumont Library, which has been through several incarnations. Used as a classroom today and here in 1917, it was at one time the staff common room. The key was once unwittingly left in the door before a meeting of the SCR, resulting in one opportunistic boy imprisoning the entire common room at his mercy. The story goes that their captivity was enduring.

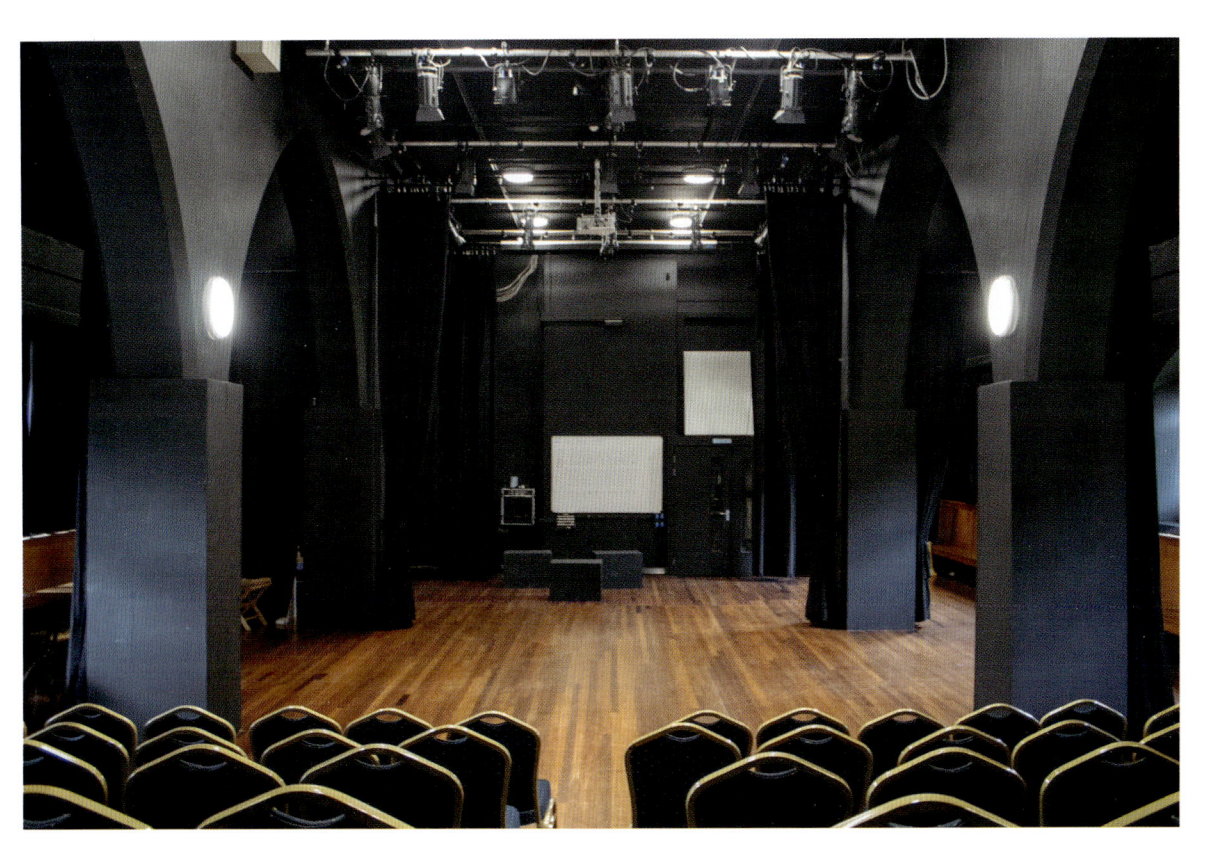

Big School now is a performance space and still very much a room at the College's heart.

Likewise, few rooms across the Quad have stayed precisely the same. Even today, as shown by the renovation of this geography classroom, there is an eagerness to ensure the College's provision is progressive and future-proofed.

OCTOBER

The classroom of 2025 hopes to be a place of greater independence, dynamism, and innovation. Students lead their learning with a far greater ownership and technology takes a supporting role. Teachers aspire for that balance between tradition and evolution.

OCTOBER

In fact, Bradfield is a leader in creating 'classrooms of the future'. It is at the forefront of learning through Virtual Reality and pioneering in its approach to the digital world.

OCTOBER

Not that we should dismiss the efforts of the past. Here, a science lab in 1917 shows a scene of great endeavour.

OB Martin Ryle, the Nobel Prize winning physicist, studied in these labs.

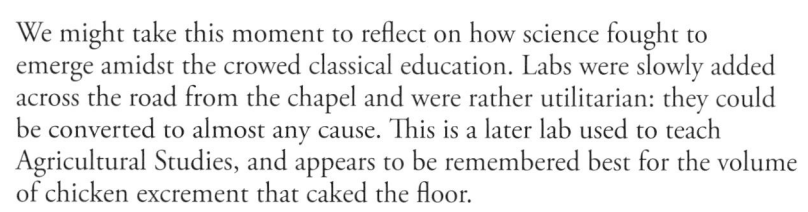

We might take this moment to reflect on how science fought to emerge amidst the crowed classical education. Labs were slowly added across the road from the chapel and were rather utilitarian: they could be converted to almost any cause. This is a later lab used to teach Agricultural Studies, and appears to be remembered best for the volume of chicken excrement that caked the floor.

The chemistry labs were amongst the last to be built, and also the very last to give up blackboards and chalk.

Bradfield's labs are now state of the art, but this scene of experimentation still echoes that of 1917.

OCTOBER

Certainly, the emphasis on enjoying one's learning seems to have grown. Learning is about more than facts and figures; if learning can be a joy, then it can be lifelong.

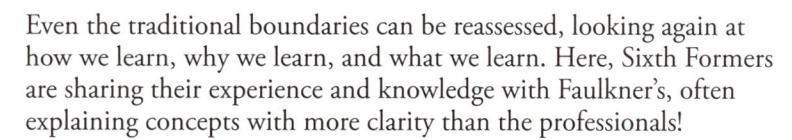

Even the traditional boundaries can be reassessed, looking again at how we learn, why we learn, and what we learn. Here, Sixth Formers are sharing their experience and knowledge with Faulkner's, often explaining concepts with more clarity than the professionals!

And some types of classrooms have ceased altogether. The Machine Shop may now be redundant, but it reminds us of a more industrial age.

Indeed, it was Headmaster Gray who made the truly vatic introduction of such advances into the classical education of the College. Fortuitously, this prepared Bradfield to do its bit in the war effort in ways Gray could never have foreseen.

Of course, not all learning happens in a classroom. The world may be your teacher, but the College no longer holds lessons in the middle of the road.

However, the College does have an outdoor classroom, complete with solar charging. Note the burgeoning Leavers' Wood behind, where students are invited to plant a tree before they leave the College.

Incidentally, this is yet another unchanged view, save for the tarmac.

Of course, it is not just the fabric of classrooms that has changed. Hailz-Emily Wringley, here being interviewed, became the first female teacher at Bradfield College in 1985. The first female governor will join in 1987, and the first housemistress in 1997.

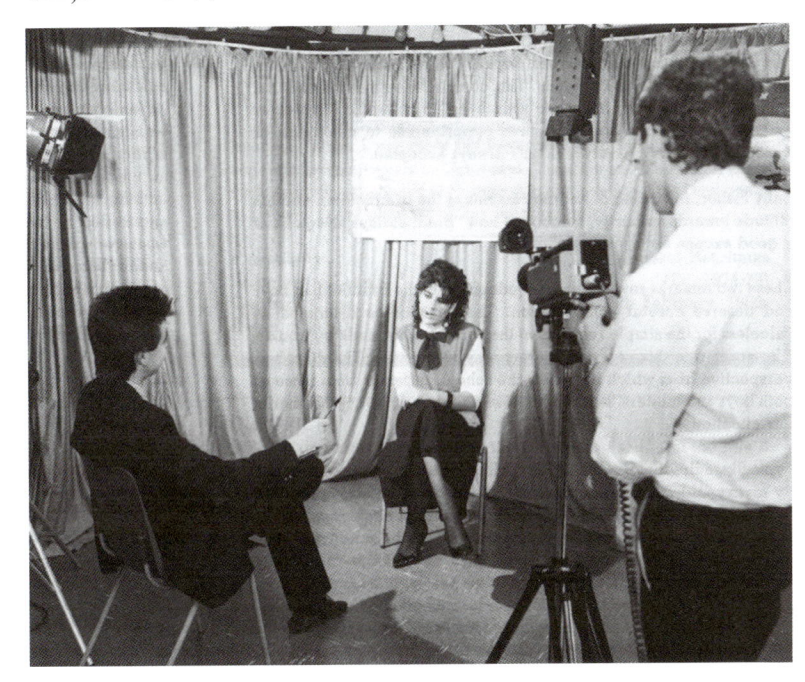

This brings to mind another great change in the College's history, namely the introduction of girls. See some of the first arrivals posing triumphantly with a redundant sign. The first girls' house, Palmer, was opened in 1989; however, girls had attended the College for almost a decade by that point, some even living with married masters' families. As it happens, three lodged with the headmaster!

Some of Bradfield's first girls in the autumn of 1979.

See the bravery of these two debating in a boys' world back in 1981! Sarah McCann (pictured) was the first girl to be in a Greek Play.

OCTOBER

Perhaps things have changed less than one thinks. The Movember fundraiser of 2010 prompted a recreation of the adjacent from 1900. And, although the modern barbigerous efforts seem rather puny by comparison, the two common rooms share a legacy of caring for and educating the pupils at Bradfield College.

The masters of 1900 sit in rather more homogenous dress and with a greater seriousness. The man at the centre is Herbert Gray, the headmaster who created Greeker.

OCTOBER

It must be said that October is not all work and no play. Students continue to excel in all fields, such as taking on the International Club of Great Britain on our clay courts. Bradfield is one of the country's preeminent tennis schools, with its cavernous indoor tennis centre being opened by Tim Henman.

# NOVEMBER

## REMEMBRANCE AND THE MILITARY

Sooner than you think, the world and its future will be yours to shape and make. Every generation has its particular challenges. Yours will too, as has your parents' generation and as has mine. I don't know what your challenges will be. They are likely to be as difficult, and dangerous, as in previous generations. But the world is a single community – we cannot escape responsibility for what happens or for failing to prevent it. Nor can we ignore our obligation to other people elsewhere. Inaction is a decision to allow evil to succeed; it has moral consequences. We cannot do better than to remember what past generations have done for us, note where they failed, and learn from and draw on their experience to make the world a better place.

**Vice Admiral Sir Jeremy Blackham (OB, E-61)**

November brings with it a marked change in spirit. The days darken, the pitches become sodden, and the mists crawl up the valley. Moreover, thoughts turn to Remembrance, and minds are cast back into the past. For the College, the tone is more sombre and reflective.

NOVEMBER

As the Sunday draws closer, various departments, houses, and services begin to remember in their own ways. Below, pupils plant small crosses in Remembrance week.

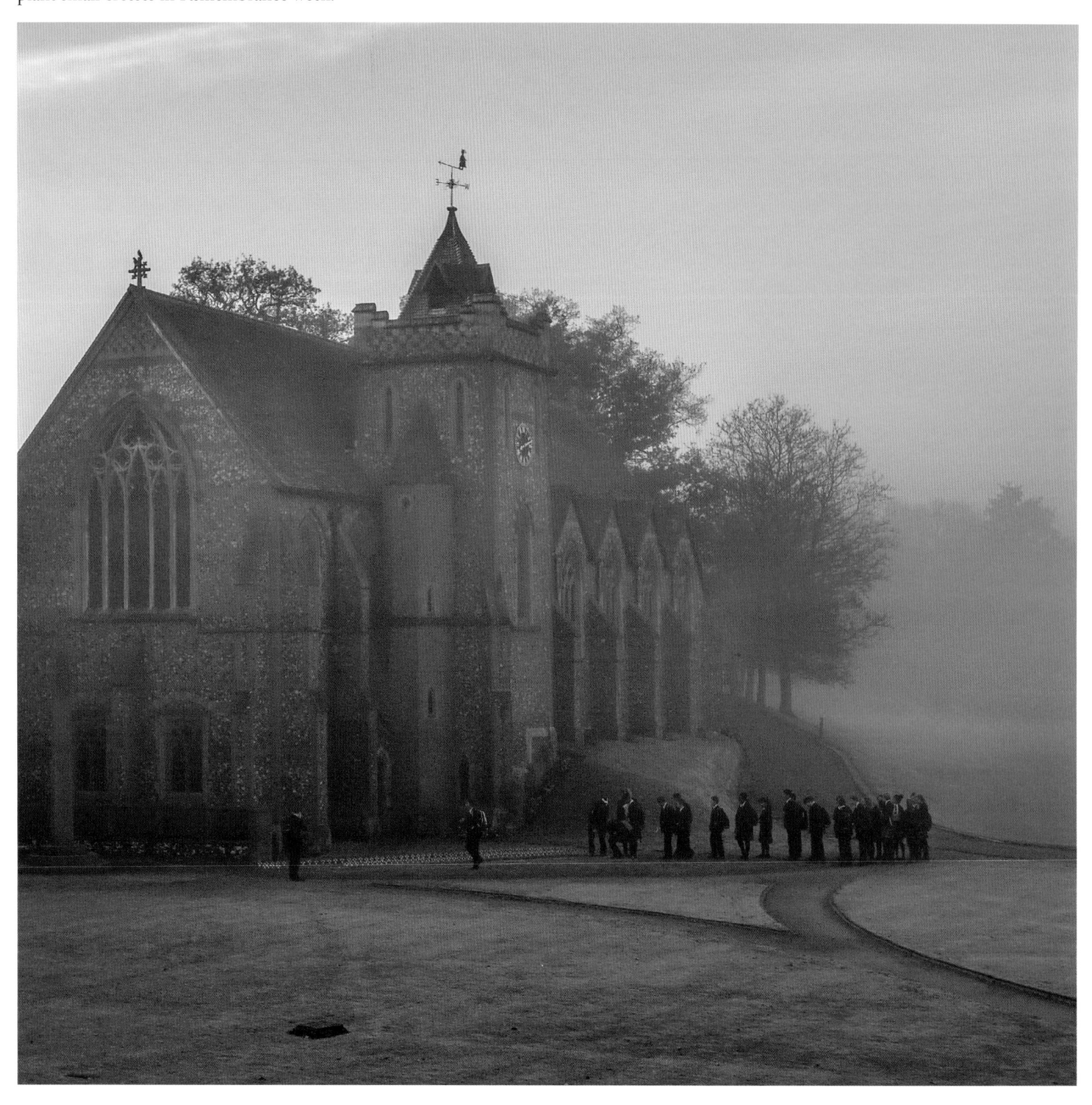

Bradfield has a proud tradition of military service, with many making the ultimate sacrifice.

A number of Rifle Corps inspections are pictured here, all in 1916. One is caused to wonder at the fate of these boys, whether it be they serve in this war or the next.

NOVEMBER

The College continues to take pride in its drill and inspections, and the lessons of discipline and respect remain vital. However, these students have a luxury beyond their forebears of 1916: that their CCF experience can be one of enjoyment and betterment, rather than a prologue to warfare.

A student receives the Annual Award for Best Army Cadet during the Biennial Inspection.

The Bradfield Rifle Corps stand for inspection in 1918. War looms large for these young men.

In 1948, the College was proud to welcome Lord Montgomery, who came to inspect the CCF. He played pivotal roles in the leadership of D-Day and the North African Campaign. Here he walks with Headmaster Hills.

Old Bradfieldian and Admiral of the Fleet Bruce Fraser (1st Baron Fraser of North Cape) also inspecting the CCF. He commanded the Royal Navy force which sunk the German battlecruiser Scharnhorst at the Battle of the North Cape on 26 December 1943. He also signed the Japanese peace treaty on behalf of the United Kingdom.

NOVEMBER

The Rifle Corps training of 1918 continues. St Andrew's Church in the background shows a constancy that belies the immediacy of European darkness.

Today, the CCF still equips hundreds of Bradfieldians, most of whom will never go to war. But they are readied for hardship, forced into resilience, and emboldened to work with others. And all this with a smile on their faces!

The Bradfield Rifle Corps rehearse their marching drills in 1918. Again, there is an ineluctable shadow over such photographs. The OTC would not be founded for another two years.

The friendships formed can feel unlikely as pupils of different ages, interests, and houses are thrown together into adversity.

The Rifle Corps was established in 1883 at Bradfield. By 1884, shooting was well-ingrained into College life, and in 1887 the Benyon family of Englefield Hall created butts (targets against a bank) with a gift of land.

NOVEMBER

Bradfield's shooting tradition is very fine. In fact, it is the view of many that Bradfield is the best shooting school in the country, and thus seated high amongst the global pantheon. One need look no further than the trophies that span our myriad victories.

The armoury as was is bustling with honours boards. This section (far right) is dedicated just to the Ashburton victors. Many have since shot for Great Britain.

Bradfield competing at Bisley in 1904. Bradfield shots rarely return empty-handed.

The 1910 Shooting Team sit around the Ashburton Shield, a trophy which frequents the College cabinet.

Bisley again, now in 1948. Our clay shooting is also excellent.

NOVEMBER

The trophy haul from 2022 alone.

Bisley in 2021

Ashburton in 2023

NOVEMBER

The OTC prepare to fire and manoeuvre. These photographs, though framed by Berkshire beauty, bear the eerie shadow of scenes just across the Channel.

Finally, it is time for parading and strategy. The Signalling Section rehearse the skill of careful measurement needed on the Western Front.

NOVEMBER

Careful strategy is also needed for the Gun Run, yet another feature of our martial past bestowing new skills and values to the modern student.

NOVEMBER

Over the many years of its history, Bradfield's Officer Training Corps, (the Junior Training Corps from 1941) has conducted many imaginative and demanding training exercises. One of the most thrilling occurred during the summer of 1946, when seven agents of the JTC's Intelligence Section were tasked with breaking a ring of hostile spies which stretched from North Wales to Sussex. The spies, who were also drawn from the school, were deeply embedded in British society and were well placed to pass sensitive information across the Channel to a hostile power.

The spy-catching operation was directed by the Intelligence Section's 'backroom boys' from a London flat. Bradfield's seven agents were relaxing at home during their summer holidays when activated, and they immediately set out to neutralise the enemy cell, hitch-hiking in uniform but switching into civilian clothes as they closed in. Armed with dummy .45 calibre revolvers, their first mission, to recover classified maps held by a woman in Marylebone High Street, London, was easily accomplished.

They were then led to their second target, a glamorous young woman living in a country house near Evesham, by messages concealed in a curtain found at 52 High Street, Oxford. She proved extremely difficult to locate, but when traced, two agents watched her house from a tree they had climbed in the garden. Once she had returned from having her hair done in Cheltenham, the Bradfield agents stormed the house, overcoming the guards after a short but fierce gun battle. The beautiful enemy spy was locked in a pantry while the agents recovered a bundle of documents vital to national security.

Subsequent missions did not always proceed flawlessly, but complications were inevitable given the unpredictable nature of espionage work and the limited intelligence available to the Bradfieldians. Near Conwy Castle in North Wales, in search of two spies, the agents nearly attacked a farm which they had erroneously identified as their lair. A disastrous confrontation with an irate farmer and his wife was avoided by a chance encounter with the spies, themselves in search of the JTC agents. The leader of the spy ring, 'the man at the top – the brains behind it all', now intervened to ensure the success of a plot to blow up the bridge spanning the River Conwy at Tal-y-Cafn. After a nail-biting series of manoeuvres and counter-manoeuvres, a spy climbed along the bridge's girders, laid two explosive charges and detonated them, before being shot by a JTC operative.

After six days of mentally and physically exhausting travel, pursuit of clues, deceptions, and cat-and-mouse chases, the exercise was called off that evening. Spies and agents, formerly bitter enemies, were reconciled over a meal together. They swam in the River Conwy, built a fire, and watched the turn of its tide.

NOVEMBER

See JCT boys train in and around the Pang, facing any obstacle whilst smoke grenades are thrown at them. Although clearly dangerous and a far cry from modern sensibilities, these photos were taken during the Second World War, and thus staff had a duty to prepare these boys for the front.

Remarkably, such scenes can still be seen in the Pang today, albeit with a risk assessment.

NOVEMBER

Such 1940s JTC training as has been mentioned continues.
Iron Bridge has certainly seen many come and go.

Of course, these photos also bring to mind the peace of our current setting, the oneiric Pang now unspoiled by thoughts of war. Tatiana Brown of the Lower Sixth captured this moment.

The OTC relax at Aldershot. A highlight in the martial calendar, Aldershot is where the great public schools would gather to rehearse manoeuvres in greater numbers.

Nor were the boys idle once training was over. During the wars the industrial equipment of the College was turned over to munitions-making. Here, proud Bradfield boys stand severely with the shells that they have made. The year was 1916 and these were sorely needed at the Western Front.

In that same vein, here Bradfield's Engineering department is called into action during the First World War.

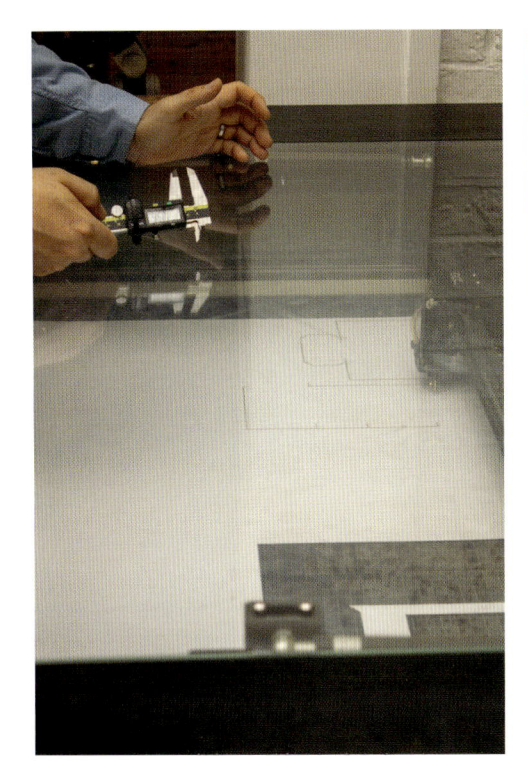

The Design department of today still rumbles and rattles with innovation, but the laser cutters and 3D printers now serve the students' creativity and imagination, rather than the necessities of conflict.

A hovercraft club was even spawned out of the department, raced here by the students who designed and built them!

NOVEMBER

Neither were the staff at Bradfield content to hide within the idyll during those dark hours. On the right, Mrs Oliver, a Bradfield matron, lends her assistance to the wounded at Englefield House, which was requisitioned into a hospital.

Indeed, a stray German bomb once almost hit the College, but instead saved us the trouble of digging another crater in our golf course.

Needless to say, the CCF continues in rude health, and students still learn those selfsame values of courage and resourcefulness. The post-imperial tone of peacetime does, however, create a real contrast between the College's military role now and that of the height of empire. That being said, two OBs, Allan Havelock-Stevens and John Charles Sanderson, have selflessly given their lives for their country post-WW2.

A student receives her citation as a First Sea Lord Cadet, an extremely rare honour.

NOVEMBER

And so November is the season of Remembrance at Bradfield. The College becomes a more reflective place and its consciousness less temporal. Students have plenty of occasion to observe the Cross of Remembrance as they walk across the Quad between lessons. Some may even pause to read a name or two.

Here, the cross is unveiled in 1916 during a WW1 memorial service by the Chief of the Imperial General Staff. It has since been moved towards Bloods Corridor (in 1951) where the names of the WW2 fallen surround it.

Here stands the memorial in its previous location, as with above. It is the oldest public school war memorial in the country, and was dedicated just a week after the Somme. More names had to be subsequently added to the base. Photograph from 1919.

The cross was fashioned by OB George Blackall Simonds, younger brother to the first ever Bradfieldian. He also sculpted the memorial for the neighbouring village, Bradfield Southend (right); tragically, his own son is on that memorial.

NOVEMBER

Every year, the College community gathers around that same memorial cross for a service of Remembrance and silence.

Major Daniels, once of the Royal Marines and now leading the College CCF, gives a reading, as does the headmaster. The chapel service is particularly poignant, and combines the singing of threnody with hope.

And although many Bradfieldians fought across Europe, Africa, and Asia, the Pang Valley was still with them.

A quiet but paradigmatic example of such affection is a collection of letters to Mrs B.M. Arnold, a housemaster's wife, sent by Bradfieldians during the long months of fighting and service.

This letter, from T.D. Bruce, was written during his captivity in a POW camp, namely Marlag O.

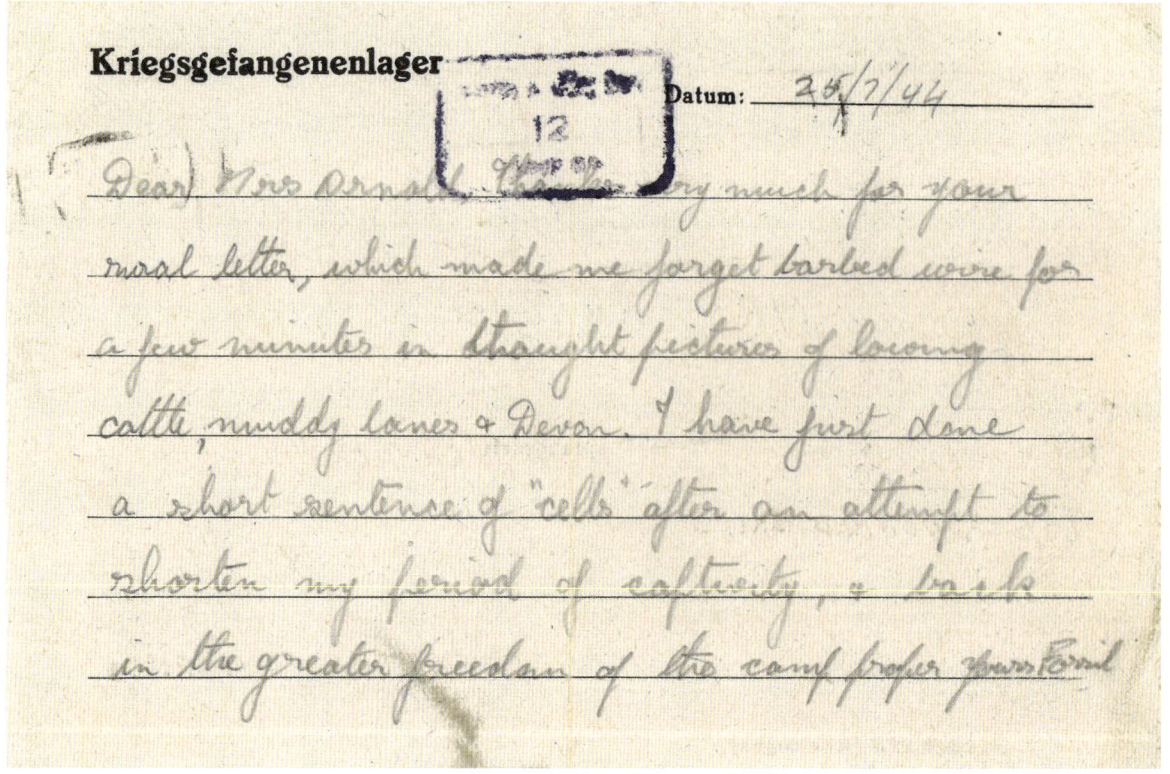

Mrs Arnold receives another letter, on this occasion from a G.C. Boolt. Note the affection he sends from Khartoum.

MRS. B. M. ARNOLD,
CANNONWALLS FARM,
WOODBURY SALTERTON,
ENGLAND. EXETER.

Sender's Address: G. C. Boolt,
P.W.D.,
Khartoum,
Sudan.

Date: 17th November, 1943.

Dear Mrs. Arnold,

This is to wish you a Very Happy Christmas from all of us, and the best of luck in 1944.

You may not have heard already, but I expect you'll be interested to know that we have now got a daughter — Julie Elizabeth, born on July 25th in Khartoum. Mother and child are both flourishing, and are now up in Alexandria, from where I have just come back after two months' leave. We had a very enjoyable, though quiet, time up there, and Julie put on a lot of weight. She has grown into an almost model child, sleeping right through the night.

I've been transferred to Khartoum from Port Sudan, and I'm now in Port Sudan collecting our furniture to send up to Khartoum. I want to get our new house properly established before Mildred returns with Julie in ten days' time. I think we shall prefer it in Khartoum, especially with the baby; I'll be working in P.W.D. Headquarters.

I hope Mr. Arnold and the family are all well, and enjoying their war-time life. I hope we'll be able to meet again next year, but I expect

A photograph of a WW1 trench from the College archive. This particular regiment was characterised by its gathering of boys from the great public schools, and many Bradfieldians would have found themselves in just such a regiment, as well as leading large groups of men in others. Although the immediate promotion of public schoolboys to officers may seem elitist to modern eyes, it must be remembered these schools provided a wealth of well-educated boys who could do drill, manoeuvre, use maps, signal, maintain equipment, pass on their OTC skills, and shoot. Public schoolboys died in horrifying and disproportionate numbers and were by no means privileged to be given their rank.

A trench map drawn by OB Gerald Clark. The chaotic nature of the Western Front, where trenches zigzagged across a shunted landscape, meant that positions shifted frequently amidst the bombardments, raids, and counter-attacks. Soldiers, often trained in reconnaissance and cartography, sketched detailed representations of no-man's-land, artillery placements, troop numbers, and enemy trench systems. This vital intelligence could then be passed to the commanding officers who oversaw the offensive and defensive operations. The accuracy and immediacy of trench maps made them essential for the survival of Clark's men.

## GERALD MAITLAND CLARK
## 1880–1916

Gerald was born on the 30 July 1880. He arrived at Bradfield College in September 1894. He played for the 1stXI cricket team and it was noted that his splendid 40 against Radley in 1899 was instrumental in bringing about victory. While at the College he won the first Wilder Divinity Prize and the Stevens' Scholarship. He then gained an Open Scholarship at St. Catherine's College, Cambridge. In 1903 he returned to Bradfield as a teacher in the Junior School and then taught in the College in 1905 specialising in Modern Languages. Gerald was responsible for the playing fields and producing wickets and was also the librarian between 1909 and 1912. When war broke out he volunteered immediately at the request of the War Office. However, it was not until March 1915 that he left his position at the College to join the 6th Battalion Northamptonshire Regiment and in the spring he gained his Majority. Gerald was killed in the Battle of the Somme at Trones Wood on 14 July 1916. His Commanding Officer wrote the following in the Northampton Independent: *'I have to mourn the loss of many gallant officers, among them was Major G. M. Clark, whose loss all the regiment will mourn. I have met no gallanter or finer soldier among the many brilliant ones the new armies have produced.'*

NOVEMBER

Oliver Woods was another of the hundreds of Bradfieldians to serve and die in the Second World War.

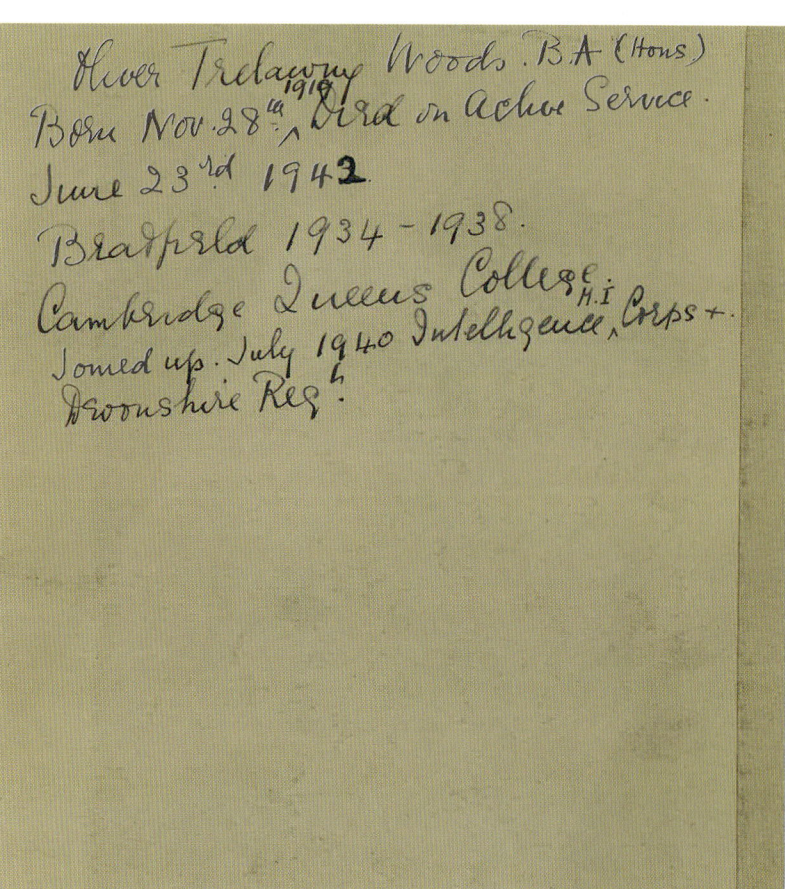

Oliver Trelawny Woods. B.A (Hons)
Born Nov. 28th 1918, Died on Active Service.
June 23rd 1942.
Bradfield 1934 – 1938.
Cambridge Queens College H.I
Joined up July 1940 Intelligence Corps +
Devonshire Regt.

The College is proud to house one of the finest First World War cross collections in the country. These markers were assembled out of anything available, and fashioned by friends of the killed soldier. All crosses pictured are Old Bradfieldians, and were largely donated by the parents of the fallen.

The headmaster holds one such cross as he delivers his reflections at Remembrance.

In World War One alone, 279 Bradfield men died and 395 were injured.

NOVEMBER

# DECEMBER

## CHRISTMAS

As December comes around and our frenetic year begins to calm, the Bradfield community gathers once again in the spiritual heart of our school to welcome the sacred season. The majestic tree, sparkling and standing tall in the sanctuary, is adorned with festive decorations, anticipating the joy of Christmas. Colours change to green and burgundy as verdant garlands gild our pillars, spreading the aroma of Christmas cheer, while the chapel door welcomes the wreath of Advent.

The enchanted choirs captivate our hearts and minds with the eternal message, as 'the word became flesh and dwelt among us'. Musicians proclaim the wonders of new life and hope, their harmonious voices and inspiring instruments heralding the good news. Generations of Bradfieldians, past and present, gather here in this timeless celebration welcoming the Christ child into our world once again and making everything new.

**Dr Rev P. Hansell, College Chaplain**

With the arrival of December comes the shine of the festive aura. The rills of the Chapel Choir flow along the corridors of the evening and everywhere trees and lights spring up. Boarding houses are converted into flashing grottos, and the term draws to a slow close. If snow comes, it brings its usual thrill of joy and chaos.

With or without snow, the weather soaks into the soil. Matches endure the valley mists, and the days feel frightfully short.

DECEMBER

But the weather can also show the College in a fresh brilliance. These photos were taken in December of 1937, but the beauty of the frost-gripped trees is no different today.

Greeker in 1979 could hardly feel further from the arcadian heights of Epidaurus.

Slipping up Hogger in the winter of 1981.

DECEMBER

Students walk to lessons in December's half-light.

A far cry from the glories of the cricket season.

DECEMBER

Whatever the weather, it is often better to be inside during December. As the days grow colder, the lights grow warmer, and the Christmas cheer begins to spread. The school draws into the chapel more and more as the skies darken, and the sacred season finds its voice.

Our Chapel Choir lead us through the great carols of winter, and delight us as we sit for their wondrous harmonies: it is when they sing alone that the numinous is most apparent.

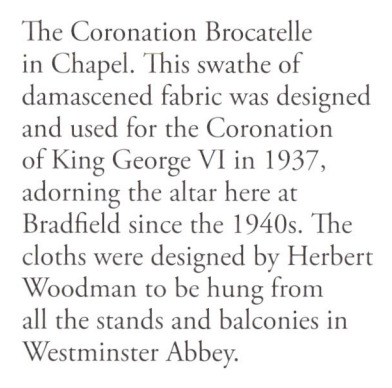

The Coronation Brocatelle in Chapel. This swathe of damascened fabric was designed and used for the Coronation of King George VI in 1937, adorning the altar here at Bradfield since the 1940s. The cloths were designed by Herbert Woodman to be hung from all the stands and balconies in Westminster Abbey.

The choir share their sacred music in the candlelight.

DECEMBER

The oncoming holidays and promise of Christmas bring a unique merriment, felt as much by these Bradfield skaters and sledgers one hundred years ago as our students today. The village smells of woodsmoke and all the windows glow.

Sledging on the flats of House-on-the-Hill.

And here, students skate on Englefield pond, the adjacent estate to the College.

And so the calendar year draws to a close, all amidst carolling and gift-giving. As a final hurrah, the Army boys launch a frosty enfilade, and others pose by their Quad Giant.

DECEMBER

# JANUARY

## SOCIETIES AND MUSIC

"In the early 1990s the College SCR contained a serious wine-tasting crowd, one of whom brought along a bottle to a post-GCSE exam class and, without opening it, led an erudite discussion about French wine. As a self-professed curious teenager, Will's interest in beyond the curriculum education was piqued and he signed up for no fewer than eight societies. His many passions outside the classroom included: philosophy, jazz, fives and religion, all of which he states gave him a good foundation in life and earned him the moniker 'The Society Baron'. But it was Bradfield's sophisticated wine society La Confrérie which set him on his future career path."

**Said of Will Lyons (H 89–94), renowned journalist and wine critic**

As January brings its frost to a new term, one is mindful that many cultures around the world have yet to celebrate their own new year. Bradfield is proud to be a place of welcome and is greatly enriched by its international students. This year, the College celebrated Lunar New Year, and many seized a chance to exhibit and learn about Chinese culture.

The return to school is also a reminder that the College truly comes to life in the evenings. There are endless societies; so many, in fact, that the College holds an annual fayre where students can encounter them all. Pictured is the Poetry Society discussing an original composition by one of its student members. The society was recently invited to dine with Louis de Bernières to discuss his work.

JANUARY

The oldest societies at Bradfield are the Shakespeare Society and Debating Society, both founded in 1854.

In that rich tradition, see here a poem by John Blackie, written to mark the centenary of the College. He places the first boy beside the Pang, and hauntingly evokes the ghosts of the Bradfieldians yet to be.

---

**70 THE BRADFIELD CHRONICLE**

## Centenary

In spite of the Editors' wish to keep the cat firmly enclosed in the bag, many Old Bradfieldians will have just cause for complaint if they are kept too much in the dark about the intended Centenary Celebrations on June 23rd-25th.

ON FRIDAY, JUNE 23RD, there will be the usual summer meeting of the Warden and Council in the morning. The rest of the day will be a half-holiday. The School will play the S.C.R. on Pit and the judges will inspect the Hollowell Exhibition and award the Prizes.

ON SATURDAY, ST. JOHN BAPTIST'S DAY, there will be no School work after morning Chapel. Visitors will then be able to see the usual Commemoration "side-shows," Hollowell, Drawing Schools, Carpenters' Shop and, this year, a special Exhibition of old Bradfield prints, drawings and documents. At mid-day there will be a Fencing Match in the Quadrangle when the School will fight a team of Old Bradfieldians. There will be a luncheon party for the official guests.

The chief event of the day will be the performance in the Greek Theatre, probably at 3 p.m., of a "Bradfield Fantasy" entitled "A Midsummer-day's Dream." Like most dreams it defies description, but it may be said to attempt the following: To pay tribute to the great men of the past and present; to give Cecil Bellamy a chance to show his genius for farce as well as for comedy and tragedy; to combine Greek Play and Shakespeare in a single theme; to let former "stars" of the Bradfield theatre speak at least a few of their original lines from stage or orchestra; to suggest something of the spirit of the Place and of its influence on all, old and young; and, of course, to provide good entertainment.

In the early evening there will be a short thanksgiving service in College Chapel, especially intended for those who cannot attend the service on Sunday morning. The Choir will lead the singing and there will be enough senior boys to ensure that volume of sound, which is so marked a feature of all services in School Chapels.

As darkness approaches, the buildings will be floodlit and there will be some singing by Choir and Glee Club. Finally, when it is dark enough, there will be fireworks across the Pang. The banks above Maximus and Major will provide the grandstands. The fireworks will be loosed off near the Pavilion on the marshes.

Throughout the day there will be a large tent for visitors, where they can get lunch, tea and supper, we hope. We also hope that there will be fine weather.

ON SUNDAY, JUNE 25TH, there will be a Centenary Thanksgiving Service in Chapel at 10.30 a.m. The Sermon will be preached by the Rt. Reverend Bishop Claude Blagden, O.B.

### FEBRUARY 4, 1850

(The first boy entered was Blackall Simonds. . . . He was admitted on February 4, 1850. . . . For some weeks he was the only Bradfield boy.—*History of Bradfield College*, Leach, p. 65.)

The boy who walked solitary by the river
Waiting for the others to come, himself
The whole Bradfield, the only Bradfieldian,
Held for a moment in his brain that winter
The whole future, the century, the six thousand.

Over the water meadows February mist hung,
Down through Barn Elms the wind blew
Roaring from Dark Entry and the hills,
The weir thundered and the willows and honey-
    suckle
Broke into green and the bricks warmed in the
    sun.

All of us were to know this and remember it,
Unshared, unguessed, he had it to himself
That first February till the others came.
What the School was to be was in his grasp
The six thousand were ghosts at his command
And as the carriage crunched on the gravel
Breaking the hush of a spring morning
Bringing the next boy, it seemed that time
Ripened not destroyed, that in 1950
The world, like Bradfield, would not have altered
    much.
                                        JOHN BLACKIE.

---

### HAT BAND

Its just a hat band, some may say,
But there are hat bands with a way
Of speaking through the colours they
In many varied forms display.

So this one tells of hopes and fears
Remembered still from youthful years:
Exultant triumph, inward tears
From wounds of mocking failure's spears.
It speaks of friends of Now and Then,
Recalling where and how and when
They lived or died. Boys grew the men
I see no more or meet again.

It speaks of hallowed abstract things
Borne down the years on silent wings:
Rehearsing memories, it sings
A tinctured psalmody that brings
Enhanced awareness of this Day
Of Change: old icons fade away;
New craftsmen mould the living clay;
New scenes enact the ageless play.

Where love no alteration finds,
Past precepts thrive in present minds.
Its just a hat band but it binds
The heads and hearts of divers kinds.

And a moving poem written by Piers de Bernières-Smart (D 38–42) whilst a student. His son, Louis de Bernières, of *Captain Corelli's Mandolin* fame, would join Bradfield as the next generation.

Not all these societies are run by staff, of course. Experts from far and wide come to share their passions, including OBs. Left is Will Lyons (H 89–94) who discovered his love for wine through Bradfield's wine society, La Confrérie, returning to give staff, students, and parents a taste for the finer things in life.

JANUARY

When Covid struck, societies became seemingly impossible to run. And, yet, things find a way, and the College was still able to 'meet' and enjoy the community that exists outside of lessons. As shown, not even hymn singing could be thwarted by a global pandemic.

Here I am, Lord. Is it I, Lord?
I have heard You calling in the night
I will go, Lord, if You lead me
I will hold Your people in my heart

Often, the daytime lessons produce work outside of themselves, and spark passions not catered for within a curriculum. Above, for instance, are the 'BRAFTAs', with students enjoying and encouraging the film work of others.

Indeed, 20 years of film at Bradfield was recently celebrated, complete with an excellent showcase of student work.

JANUARY

As for past societies, the students had far less to occupy them in evenings gone by. The modern student is pulled in all directions, but the absence of technology and constant co-curricular left far more time for leisure a hundred years ago. Here, for instance, the boys of House-on-the-Hill wile away the later hours of 1917 in reading. At least they had the comfort that chapel was generally twice a day! They are sitting in 'Meads', their dining hall.

But the boys were also capable of making their own fun. This is the 1917 Wireless Society. Both these photos, with boys crowded round the newspaper and the radio, have echoes of the ongoing war they would have been so cognisant of.

O.B.B. Day.

F. Wilson -18

In a way, the jam-packed society culture on this current scale can be seen as something of a modern innovation. As had been said, 175 yeas ago, the boys were left largely to their own devices when the evenings came around. Having to entertain themselves, they might choose to fill the time by sketching their masters as various aquatic animals, as was done here by Frank Wilson in 1918.

One College history records boys in a histrionic frenzy about the release of a new edition of Byron. Their eagerness to get to the bookshops of Oxford by any means serves to demonstrate the role literature played in those long evenings.

At least the first motorcar to ever enter the village caused some entertainment.

JANUARY

Bradfield's TV station, Diamond TV, was once run out of this rather unglamorous building, known as 'The Moat'. The great aerial that once thrust into the sky has gone, and The Moat is now used for deliveries and such. Bradfield TV came to an inauspicious end when the police were called after the locals kept tuning in to what they presumed was pirate television!

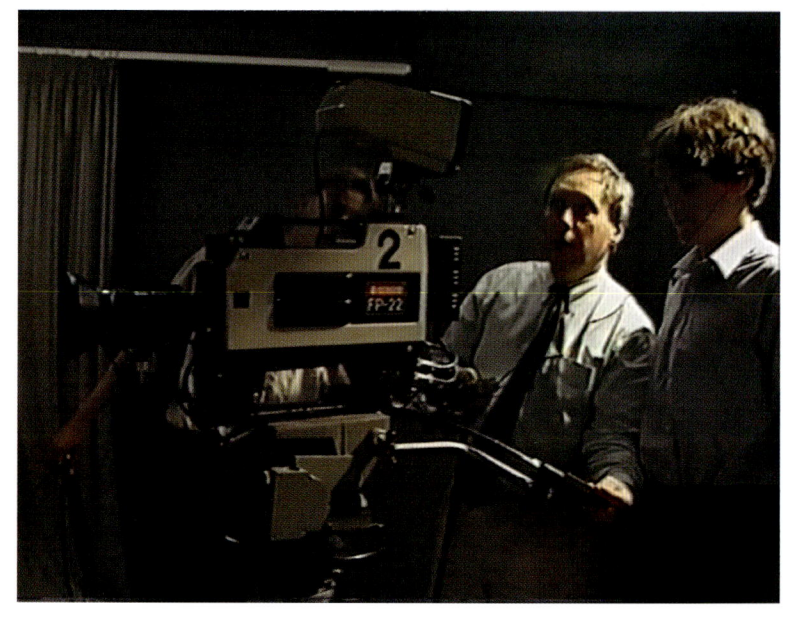

Mr D. Lomas, master of Physics, helps the students in their studio.

And, of course, when not hearkening the call from any particular society, one can always enjoy a dance. It is hard to detect the theme in this rather dingy-looking 1983 affair.

On the subject of nightlife, the social space where sixth formers can chat over a glass of beer or wine has bounced all around the College. Even the School Shop once played host to 'Blundells', the name of the student bar, but now the evening drinks are held in the refurbished Stunt Pavilion (below).

JANUARY

JANUARY

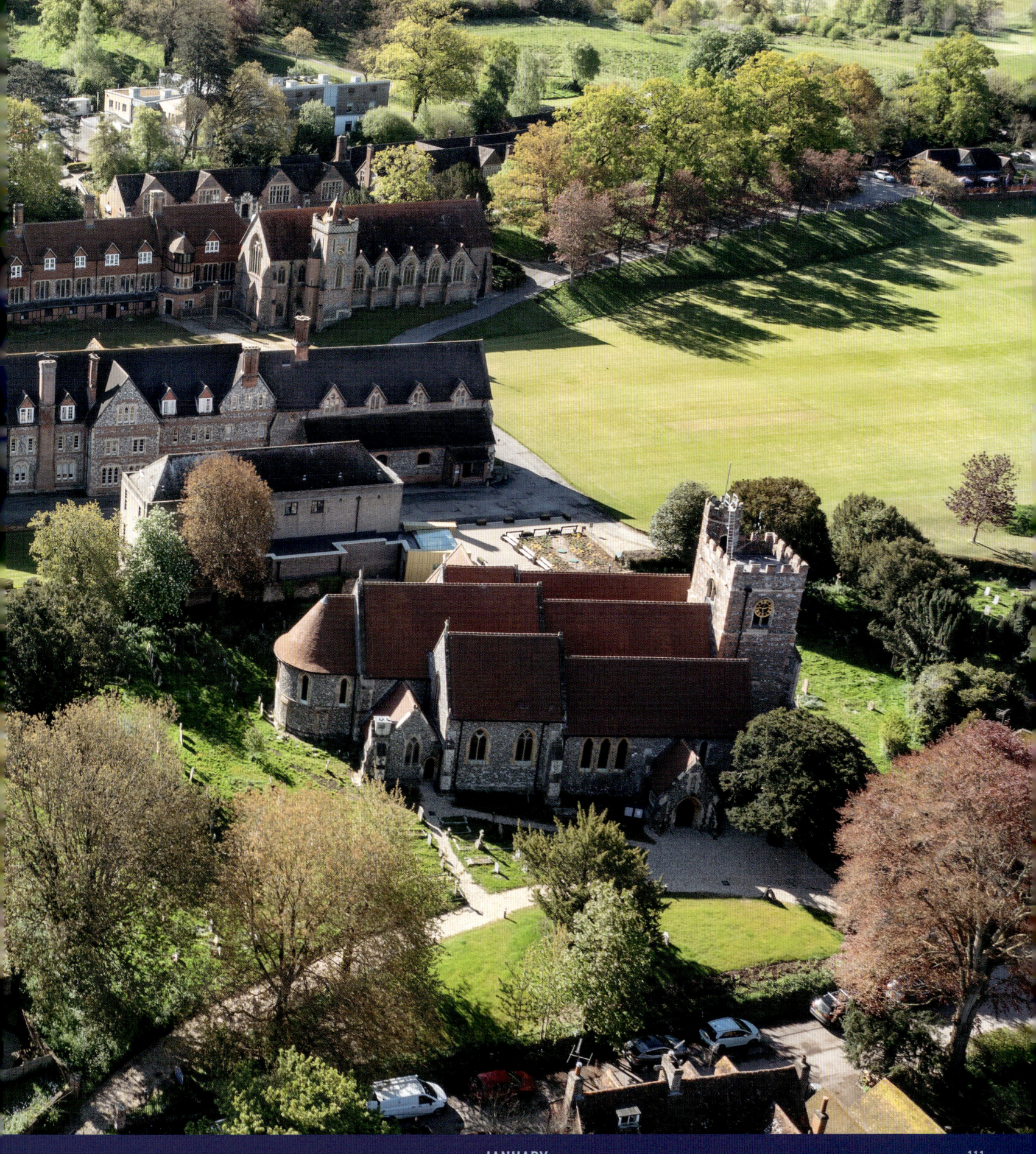

JANUARY

What is Music to Bradfield? Unapologetically, my mind leads to performances in the Music Hall, the Old Gym, the Chapel, and of course, Greeker. On their own, these spaces are merely bricks and mortar. Filled with pupils, they come alive – and never more so than when they are creating music together. In my view, the Chapel remains central to the College, and it is here where the whole school community gather to sing together every week. There is no greater communal act than raising one's voice in chorus with your peers. Where else in College life do so many participate in a single unified act at the same time? The result is astonishing – the sound of 400 young adults enjoying themselves while singing their favourite hymns. Music can be academic, it can be a personal expression, and it can be the start of a lifetime pursuit, but above all here at Bradfield, Music is the unashamed expression of joy.

**Mr D. Quinn, Director of Music**

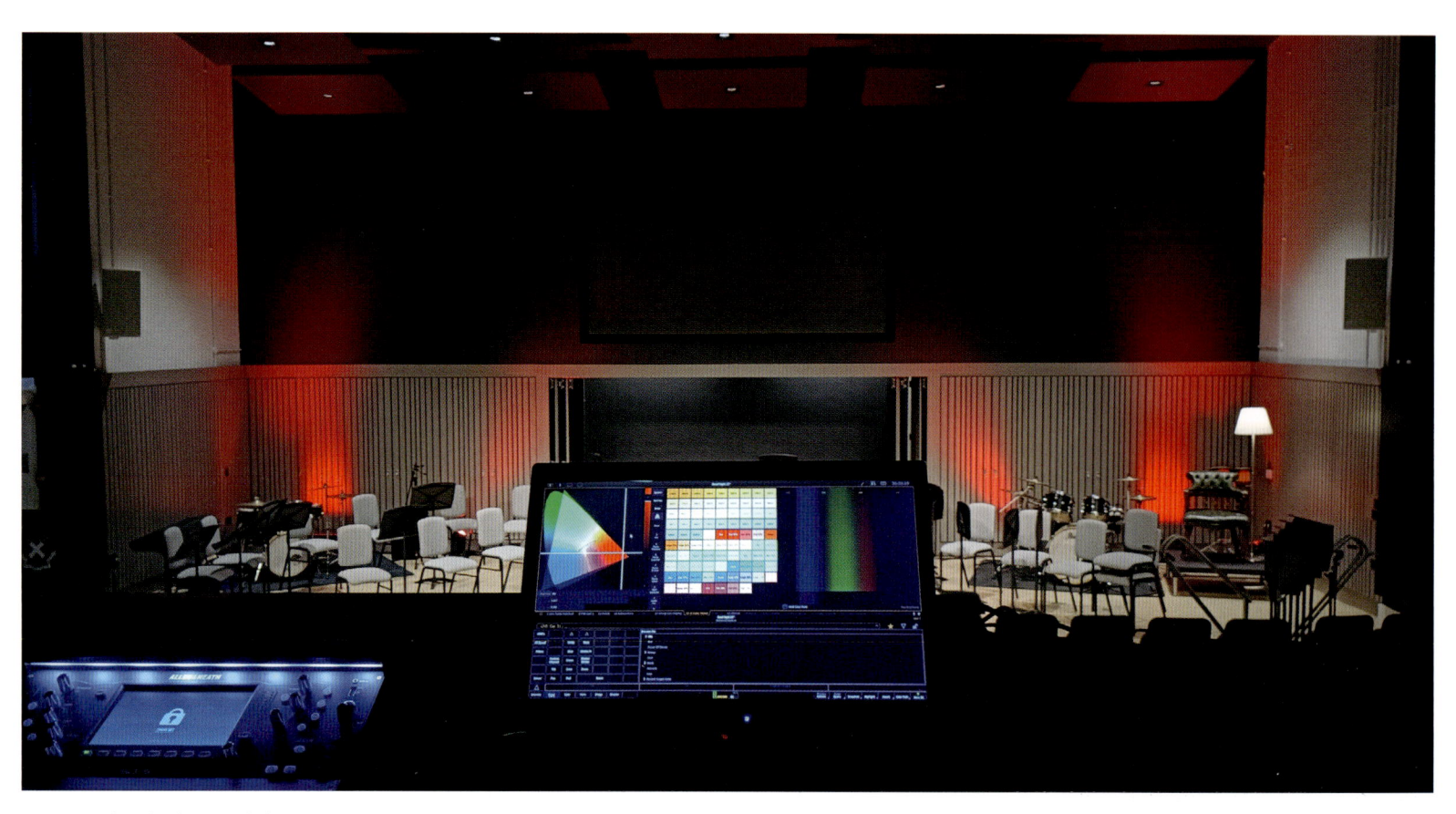

Yet, amidst the buzz of these evening societies, one of the great pleasures remains walking past the Music School and delighting in all the various sounds of rehearsal and euphony. They spill out of the summer windows and foreshadow the performances yet to come.

A greater pleasure still is when these strands combine into wonderful performances, such as our Spring Concert below.

JANUARY

Naturally, music is a pillar of Bradfield, not just in grand performance, but in daily life. Take these: a 1958 score of the College Ballad, and a 1950s copy of 'Swervers', Dr Gray's College hymn. As one sees from the lyrics, Swerver's is not particularly coeducational, and was hence dropped.

The singing of Psalm 91 has also spanned much of the College's life. Tradition has it that boys returning from matches would begin to chant the Psalm as they turned off the road towards Pangbourne and sing heartily as they drove up Common Hill. The chant ended abruptly when they arrived back at the College.

Corporate singing at Bradfield is often done several times a week, and gives the students a grounding in music, unity, and tradition.

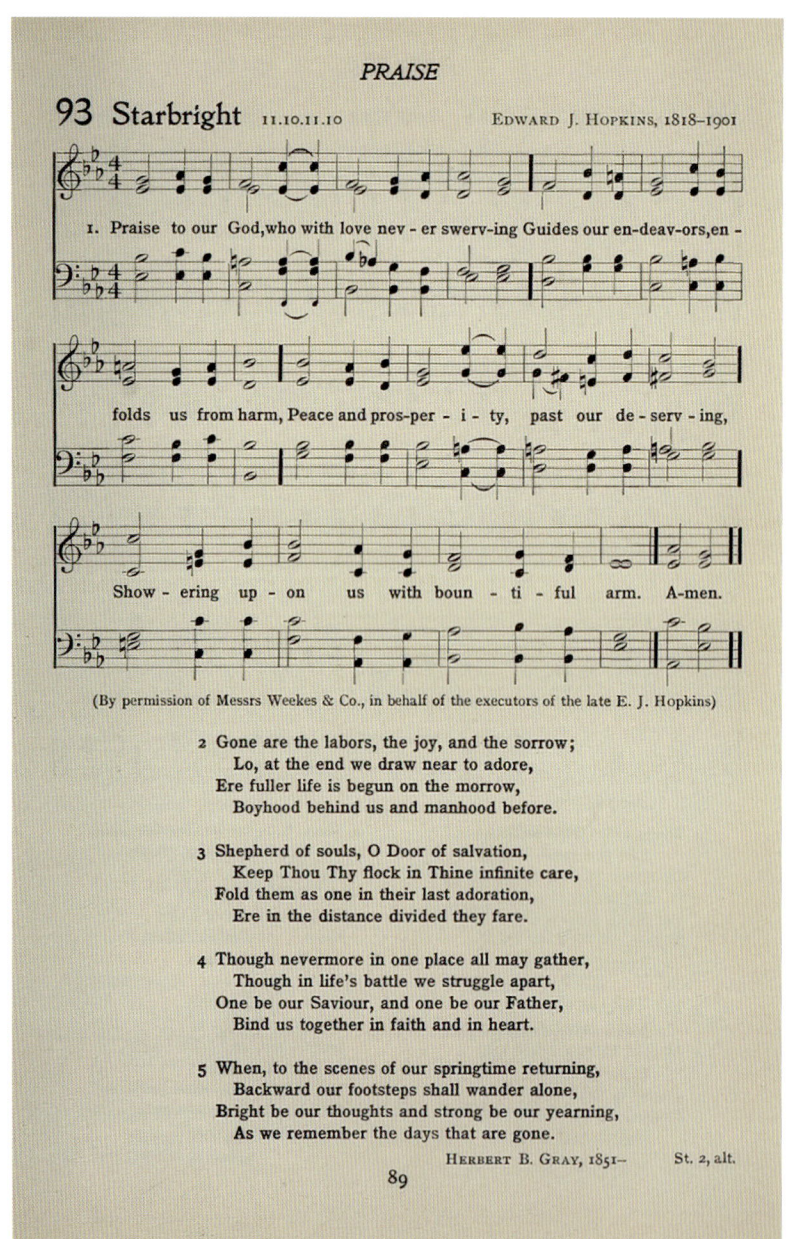

Bradfield can do the intimate as well as the grand. House Solo Instrumentals (top) is a great badge of honour to win for your house, and the Yattendon Community Concert is a way to serve and enrich the surrounding area with music.

JANUARY

In fact, the College has a real flair for contemporary music, performing sometimes in the unlikeliest venues. Pictured here, for instance, is a performance in a Pizza Express!

And these bands have a great legacy. Here, the Jazz Society rehearses.

And here, a band called Time Between.

The Duke of Edinburgh saw fit to visit the Bradfield musicians, and even sampled the students' homemade wine (made from oranges). When pushed for his views, His Royal Highness remarked that the taste was 'interesting'.

JANUARY

Other venues have a little more splendour. A performance at Englefield House serves as illustration.

Many of these great shows spring out of societies that students run themselves, with plenty disappearing off into the Music School for hours at a time. These 1909 programmes show the heritage of the musical clubs at the College.

Equally, another aspect of Bradfield's musical inheritance is how often it augments the dramatic performances of the stage. Whether it is in this performance of *Agamemnon* in 1900 or in *Twelfth Night* in 1960, the music imbues the narrative.

Every boy in the school was once required for the Greek Play, and thus many chose to be musicians.

Musicals themselves have legacy at Bradfield, particularly enabled by going co-ed.

The girls and the gangsters from *Guys and Dolls*, 1993.

*The Boy Friend*, 1998.

*Godspell*, 2018.

Our most recent musical, the 2024 *Little Shop of Horrors*.

One of the crowning moments of music at Bradfield was a recent opera, namely a performance of Purcell's *Dido and Aeneas* from 1689. It must be appreciated how few schools would dare to even attempt such a feat, and yet every note was flawless.

Music scholars play to the Pang in 2000.

JANUARY

# FEBRUARY

## ACADEMIC ENRICHMENTS

Bradfield in the evenings – magical at all times of the year but especially so in the middle of winter. The myriad possibilities in terms of academic enrichment at this time of year, when the cold and darkness envelop the College, abound. Staring at the stars through the icy winter air from the astronomy hut on Hill 2, trekking by the Pang in search of rare wildlife, congregating in Bloods for recitations of Dickens as the darkness descends, tramping down to the warmth of Art to imagine and create, listening to the wise words of guest speakers in the Music School amidst the stillness of a cold midwinter outside – there is nowhere quite like Bradfield to inspire, challenge, enhance, and enable. The life of the mind, paradoxically, is never more alive than in these so-called grim months of winter.

**Mr J. Saunders, OB and Housemaster of Stone (E)**

Alongside those societies, the evenings are also filled with constant academic enrichment. Experts and leaders come in regularly to deliver our Athena and Minerva lectures, but also, as here, to talk to the students about their welfare and their values. Above, author and speaker Patrick Foster recounts the moving tale of his recovery from a gambling addiction, and gives sage advice to our young people.

As vital as it is to enlist these regular speakers from top universities and professions, the College endeavours to give students a voice, and equip them with confidence and eloquence. Take the annual Halsted Declamations, begun in 1940, where all the Upper Sixth scholars declaim a speech to their peers. When one remembers that students frequently lead assemblies, chapel, house call, charity events, formal dinners, and much more, it is hardly a surprise that our students speak so well.

FEBRUARY

Through giving the students this voice they can teach us a great deal; for instance, February brings a season of Talks Inspiring Bradfieldians. These TIB talks give students an opportunity to explore and expound what matters to them, and to practise public speaking before an audience of their peers.

FEBRUARY

# THE SIXTH FORM CLUB REPORT 86/87

With the Sixth Form Club in the hands of the Lower Sixth in September 1986, the newly formed committee set out to organise a party, to persuade as many girls as possible to invite Bradfield to their school parties and to arrange some interesting trips.

## PARTIES-HOME

Our own 'Le Cadavre Exquis' Party, for which we took over the Village Hall, was a great success thanks to the numerous helpers and the support we received from the Sixth Form and from several members of the SCR.

The highlight of the evening was a 60 minute stint by 'Busted', the school band, comprising Paddy Oliver, Jes Farr, Ed Browning and Willie Bradford. Their performance was very impressive. One guest explained that as she stood on the dance floor, she found herself looking back and forth between the band and the disco (which was run incidentally by our very own resident DJ Mark Briggs.) to discover where the music was coming from.

## PARTIES-AWAY

The functions away, over the year, have proved to be popular and often very amusing .... 6.30, and the coach is ready, packed with the team of virile young men (including Mr Coleridge), drenched in duty-free after shave, hair caked in foul-smelling, sticky gel and all constantly asking each other whether their bow ties are straight.

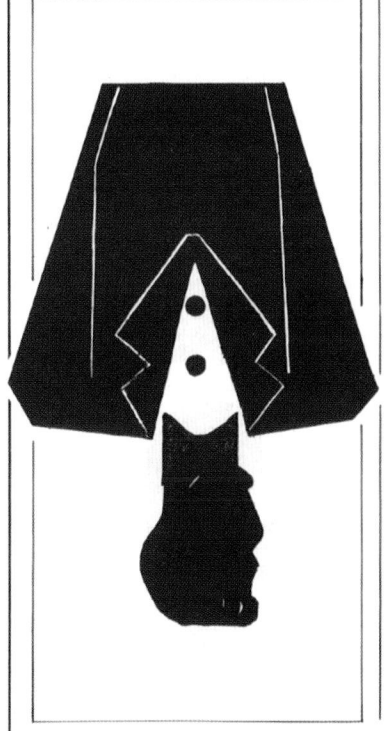

With a clean sheet away from home, the boys are confident of a good team performance and hope to score a few in the process.

On the way, if one listens carefully, ignoring Ed Browning's noisy rendition of 'Star Trekkin', the team talk of 'chat-up' lines emerges from the back seat. Bill Cairns' suggestions are laughed at, but won't be used, Guy Bullock is told to keep his voice down and someone feels it neccessary to explain to Richard Garrett that most teenage girls are unlikely to know a great deal about the fall of the Austro-Hungarian Empire.

On arrival the boys begin limbering up, with brief hair shaking and posing exercises in front of wing mirrors or reflective surfaces available.

There is no need to check the studs before kick off as they soon appear, launching themselves amidst the ladies, so smooth that no referee could possibly complain.

With some promising displays from both sides the teams ended with a draw. Fine performances were shown by Christopher Griffin, who, with the physique of a marine and the perception of an Oxbridge English student, could pick out the darlings (or Cordelias) and then handle them as if they were his rucksack; by Charles Routh, who somehow managed to remain dark, enigmatic and mysterious throughout the whole evening, and finally, by Ben Lauder, who was cautioned for an off the field incident with another player.

## TRIPS

Our first was when a dozen Bradfieldian apparitions were hastily dropped at the Hexagon theatre, by a terrified coach driver, to see 'The Rocky Horror Picture Show', a bizarre audience participation extravaganza.

Our second was to see the West End, fast-moving comedy 'When did you last see your Trousers?' The boys enjoyed it and Mr Kilburn said it was better than he'd expected it to be, so it must have been good!

## FUTURE

At the moment, with tickets already booked for trips to see Bob Dylan in concert, 'The Canterbury Tales' and some other London Shows, we are also organising 'Le Cadavre Exquis II' Party and replying to invitations.

Before I finish I would like to thank Mr Coleridge for all his invaluable help and support, and charm in 'getting things cleaned!', as well as Messrs Kilburn; Hankey, Clements and Mrs Flint.

Written by: **Jon Wood** and **Al Petrie**; Drawings by; Jon, Enoch, and Stan; Other committee members: Alex Lumby, Bill Cairns, Will Oscroft, Jim Birch, Dave Mills, Justin Clarke, Ru Callender and Ollie Chamberlain.

---

Like societies, the best academic enrichment can often be student-led. Budding journalists can create and compose for numerous College publications, whether that be for the house, sports team, club, or school event. This, of course, is nothing new. One reads this 1986 Sixth Form club report with great delight, noting the dry wit that epitomises much good writing.

**ISSUE 229**

27/09/16

SP Editors:
Ben Norris
Rory Tennant

WEEKLY BRADFIELD SPORTS PAPER

# BRADFIELD SP

Photographer:
Harry Bird

## GOOSE 2016

On that theme, the student publications are ubiquitous at Bradfield. See the front cover of a weekly sports paper, Bradfield SP, left, and the Scholars' magazine to the right.

128 — FEBRUARY

# Power

The Bradfield College Scholars' Magazine 2024

FEBRUARY

Academic enrichment is about taking a step further from what is done in 'curriculum time'. The History of Art show is a fantastic exhibition of Bradfieldian talent and endeavour, and students are expected not just to present their work visually, but also explain their own relationship to it.

FEBRUARY

Work from the 1988 Spring Art Exhibition shows the heritage of such exhibitions.

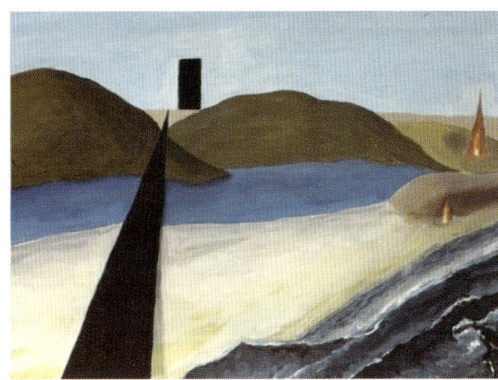

Or perhaps one is inspired to look far beyond the College. This is the second observatory built at Bradfield.

FEBRUARY

And sometimes those evenings are filled with something a little special. February of 2024 saw Bradfield triumph yet again in the ISFA cup, cementing their place at the top of the independent schools' tree. The final was played at Stadium MK, where the challenge faced by the boys was as much about resilience and composure as it was footballing skill.

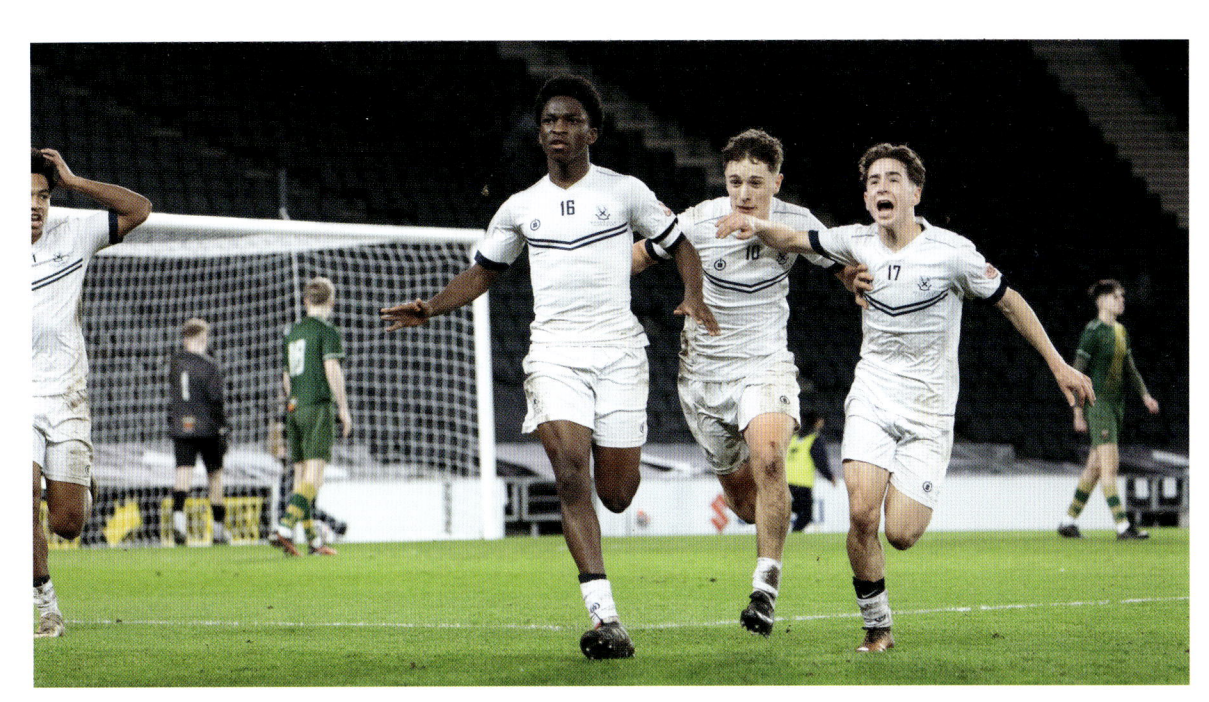

The whole school travelled to Milton Keynes to unite behind the 1st XI.

FEBRUARY

FEBRUARY

FEBRUARY

# MARCH

## THE VALLEY

I would disappear into the local fields for hours after school. Most people would think it weird sneaking up on deer, buzzards, and kingfishers, and that is why I took up photography.

**Bertie Gregory (G 06–11), cameraman on major David Attenborough nature documentaries**

The beauty of the College is circumambient. The river flows through the valley, steeped on either side with gentle hills. Woods hover above the morning mists, and trees older than the College heave up their leaves in spring.

It feels like the weather is turning. There is warmth in the sun and the grounds staff at last reap some reward for their efforts. Flowers begin to ring the fields and the Quad is finally in bloom.

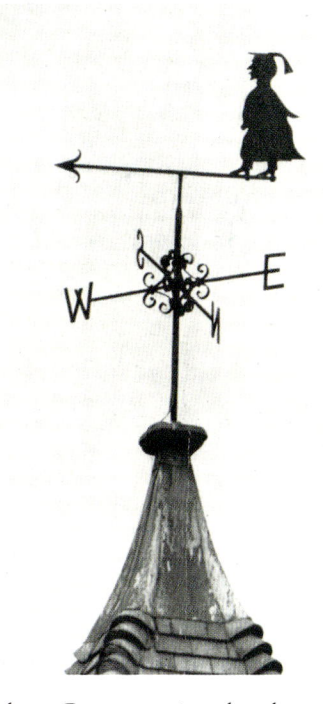

Herbert Gray, one time headmaster of the College and edifier of Greeker, sits atop the chapel weather vane where he keeps a watchful harbinger's eye for better weather. The College below him looks out, equally Panglossian.

MARCH

Ours is a stunning natural setting where the gentle rhythms of the British countryside are reflected in the slow running waters of the River Pang. The setting is not, however, just a beautiful backdrop to Bradfield's education but an intrinsic part of the learning experience. Bradfield is indeed a rural idyll, but it is also a fertile platform. The same is true of the College buildings, characterised by the long, low range round Quad, with its welcoming arms of warm red brick, steely flint, and trusty oak. Bradfield is a kind place.

**Dr C. Stevens, Headmaster**

In many ways, we are reminded once more of the joy of returning to Bradfield. The leaves and meadows which first greeted us back in September flash anew, and we know again how lucky we are.

Here, the snow drips off Hillside (F), one of the College's oldest houses. It was acquired by the College in 1878 to become a junior school with modest boarding (12 boys in 1883). For decades it was thus known as 'J.S.'.

The Junior School around 1900.

The Junior School in 1917.

MARCH

Crocker, as it exists today, is a game unique to Bradfield; more specifically, it is only played by Hillside (F). The origins and rules are equally nebulous.

Around the College, the ice yields the streams, and the Pang flows in redoubled spate. The sluice and weir rather lack their drama of old, but be comforted to know that your author risked life and limb to bring you the modern shot.

MARCH

B471. Bradfield, from the meadows.

Many here associate spring with the withdrawing of the waters and the retreat of the marshland grip. More trees have risen since this century-old photograph, but all will recognise the feel of the Water Meadows that separate New Ground from the mainland. These wetlands were bought in 1932.

Those who live here sometimes talk about the 'Bradfield light'. It morphs throughout the year, but spring gilts it with gold. These sacred moments clearly mean a great deal to the students, two of whom ventured to capture it here. These are the work of Ella Stevenson and Flora Berens in the Upper Sixth.

Given our setting, spring has been a time of ardent zoology. Take these records from 1924 depicting the various life that thrives in the valley.

MARCH

Since those photos, 101 years ago, there has been a desperate decline of wildlife nationwide. However, with environmental matters squarely in their consciousness, the students all muck in to the sustainability drive.

Take our apiary, which sells its own honey locally, as an example. Far from being a token effort, note the celebration of bees in the Thai Garden. Aside from the information delivered about bees themselves, the grounds staff had labelled various plants around the College that are favoured by pollinators, and pupils now even walk between lessons equipped with 'bee revival kits'.

Even house competitions are sustainably driven. Each house competitively grows vegetables for the College kitchens, and maximal fecundity is keenly coveted. See the variety of G House's wholesome efforts.

The fruits of their labours on the way to the kitchens.

MARCH

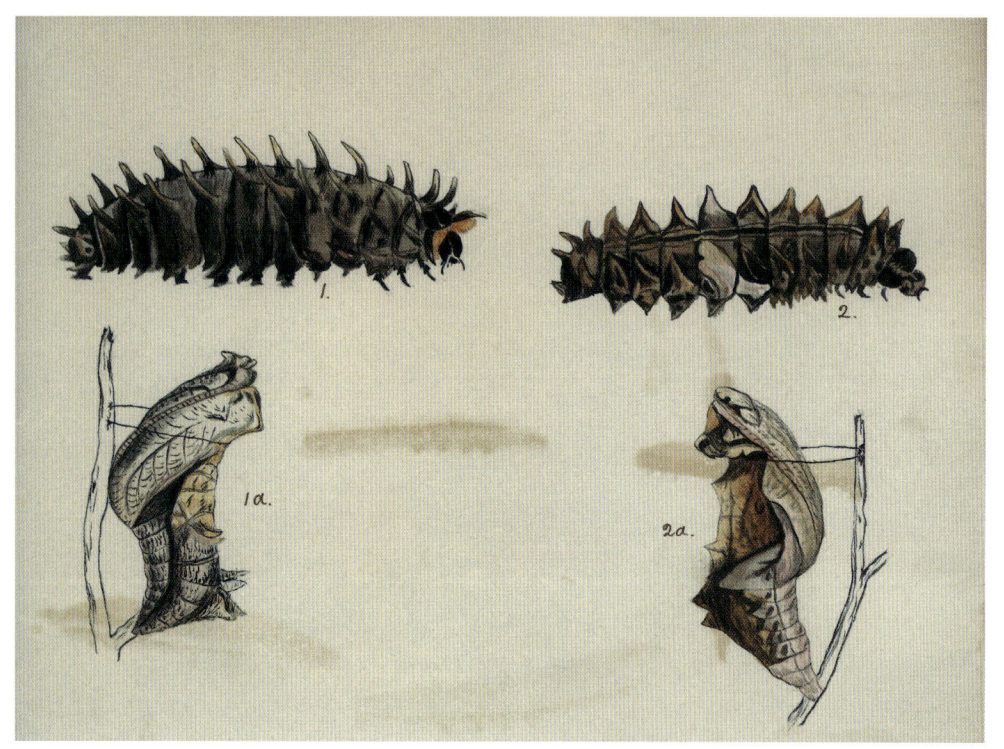

Various studies of local beasts, and a Lepidoptera, all by burgeoning student-zoologists of the past.

The College has also cared for its own animals, including a beagle pack. Here, a meet gathers outside what is now Hillside (F). These photographs were taken in 1924, and the subject is very much of its time.

MARCH

The College's profound relationship with the Pang endures. We can all hope and ensure that it continues to provide every student with a sensitivity towards and love of nature.

A pupil learns how to handle a kestrel in the 1940s. It was said that the Founder, a keen ornithologist, could summon a cuckoo to land on him at any moment.

This passion can even translate onto the international stage. OB George Blackall Simonds sculpted *The Falconer*, a piece of Bradfield now in Central Park, New York.

Incidentally, George also founded the British Falconry Society.

Boys enjoy the opportunity to canoe on the nearby Thames.

Boating on the Thames, almost 100 years earlier.

Lady Mary Thynne, royal courtier; former wife of 3rd Baron Nunburnholme, and later wife of Sir James Ulick Francis Canning Alexander; daughter of 5th Marquess of Bath, crossing the Pang.

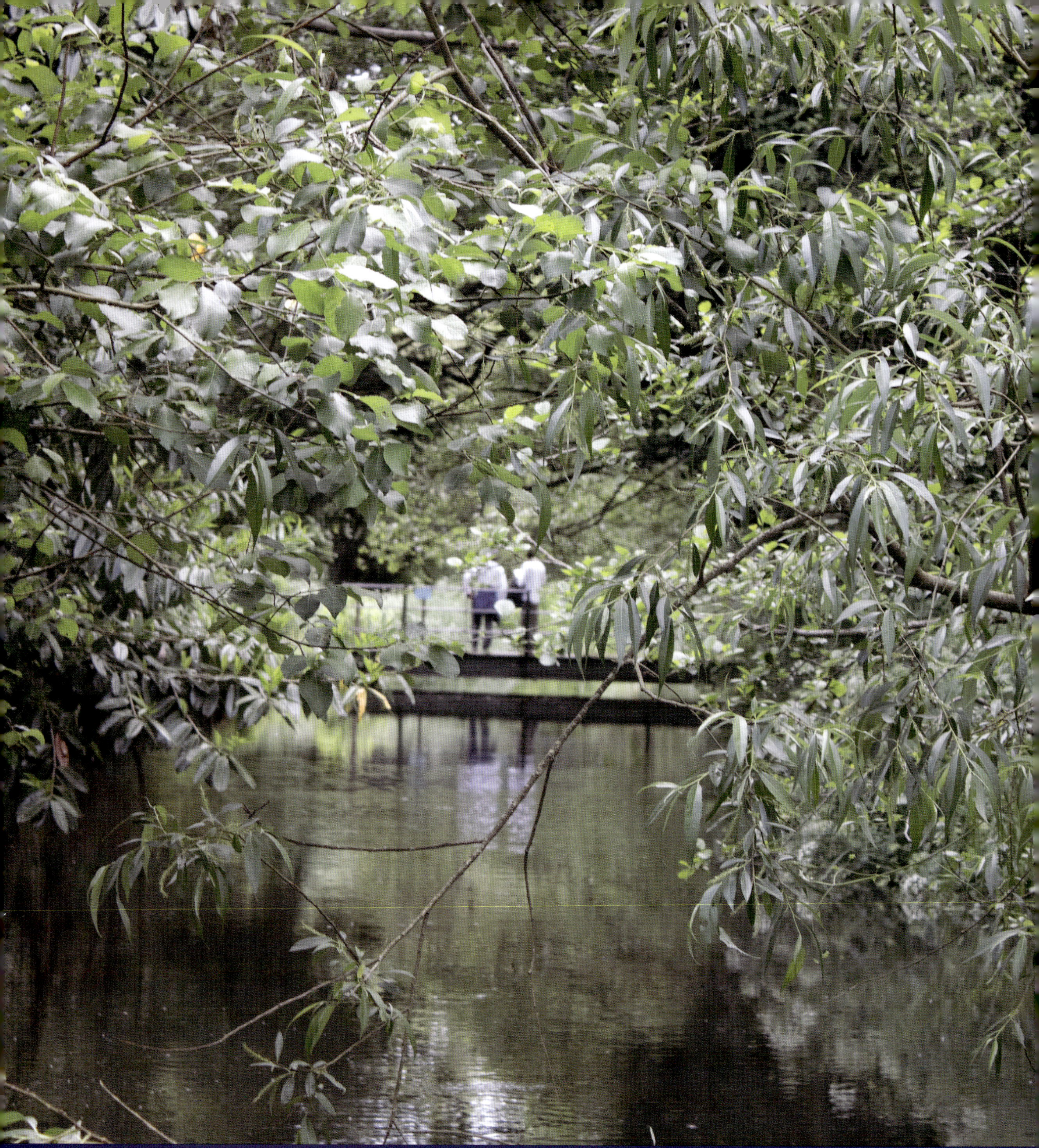

March also brings the Steeplechase, a race dating back over a century. To the left is the 1938 race, with boys bracing themselves to climb the weir.

The Steeplechase was designed to test far more than endurance. There is also a question of character, resilience, and determination.

MARCH

The waters are chilling, and try one's resolve.

MARCH

MARCH

The boys complete the parlous climb out of a local chalk pit.

The reader will be comforted to know that the modern College has taken a slightly more sensible approach to student safety. Many of the elements have endured, but the requirement to hurl oneself against anything sharp or fast-flowing has been occluded.

In times gone by, members of the Upper Sixth have even dared to run the Steeplechase in fancy dress.

MARCH

# APRIL

## PARTNERSHIPS AND OUTREACH

Our rural West Berkshire location often means that community partnership and outreach initiatives involve a minibus journey, not always the highlight of a tired teenager's school day. On the return trips, though, there is a tangible shift in their demeanour. They are happy, energised, and often humbled, especially after listening to local primary school pupils read, coaching sport at after-school clubs, or writing up life stories of retired members of the local community, a project where they gain real insight into lives lived and lessons learned. Collaborating with local schools in music concerts, CCF activities, or leadership and academic seminars, forges relationships that transcend classroom walls. And it's not just about local impact but global connections too. I have seen friendships formed when pupils in Berkshire connect online with pupils in a learning centre on the outskirts of Nairobi and I love the camaraderie that arises during impromptu dance-offs when the boys and girls from the OSCAR Foundation visit from Mumbai. These moments of connection and contribution are a testament to the power of young people to make a positive difference in the world, both locally and internationally, and they are what truly define the Bradfield spirit.

**Mrs H. Morris, Head of Partnerships**

Bradfield's partnerships are eclectic. Some span across oceans, some merely a few Berkshire fields. The College's bond with the OSCAR Foundation certainly falls into the former category, and is longstanding. The Foundation works in the slums of Mumbai to give children opportunities through football and schooling. In 2023, some of those very children were able to visit the College and learn alongside our own students.

The work of the Bradfieldians and the story of the OSCAR children was recognised by Downing Street, where both parties were invited, and a meal was later held with the patron, the Duchess of Edinburgh.

And although the historic outreach of Bradfield may not be so far-flung, it is remarkably enduring. For instance, in 1912 the College adopted the Working Lads' Club in Peckham to form the Bradfield Mission Club, seen here in 1930. As the Bradfield Club today, it helps Southwark's young people with guidance and purpose.

There had been a school mission of sorts since 1885, but the Bradfield Club was its most significant venture. With a belief in bringing the best of Bradfield's physical education to London, here is the Bradfield Club in Peckham Gym, 1910s.

And here the runners from that gym squad parade at Queen Mary's visit to Peckham, 1927.

The gym squad pose with the Club's patron, the Earl of Athlone, its founder, Major Richard Hayward, and its warden, Canon John Douglas, 1927.

The Junior Gym Team in 1913.

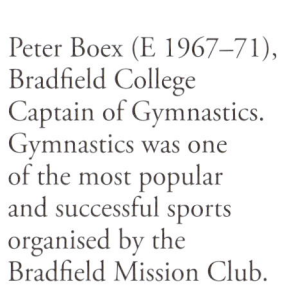

Peter Boex (E 1967–71), Bradfield College Captain of Gymnastics. Gymnastics was one of the most popular and successful sports organised by the Bradfield Mission Club.

APRIL

Not all the partnerships attract the attention of Downing Street, and often go unsung in the daily life of Bradfieldians. The Primary School Partnerships, for instance, is a quiet part of their regular service to others.

These many partnerships form a wider weekly service programme, namely 'CSP'. Students may find themselves cleaning the Greeker, maintaining the greenery, or even volunteering at a local farm.

CSV is CSP's ancestor, here hosting a hospital visit to Bradfield. From 1964, Bradfield's Community Service Volunteers worked with local charities, including the Wayland Hospital for the mentally ill, the primary school attached to it, and Southend's Evergreen Club for the elderly. The boys on the right are gardening for an elderly lady in 1973.

And here, the CSP programme takes students to serve at a local farm.

Pupils perfect the art of ensnaring poultry.

Members of the Shell maintain the farm track by filling in potholes.

A view of the College from Rushall Farm. Students also attend a weekly leadership course here as part of their CSP, often enjoyed by the fire pit.

APRIL

And here the Lenten Appeal race for charity. The Lenten Appeal continues to this day in the form of food parcels made by the students.

Naturally, the partnership with the alumni remains strong. The annual trophies, such as the Bostelmann Running Trophy, or the match against the 1st XI, are an exceptional opportunity for past to mix with present, and for the OBs to know that the College is in good hands.

A summer OB reunion helps connect the past and the present.

APRIL

# MAY

## BEGINNINGS OF SUMMER

England cricket captain Ted Dexter named Pit as one of his three favourite grounds and, in May, there can be few finer venues for the nation's summer sport. The bare branches that frame the boundary for the opening fixtures of the season are now hidden by bright young leaves and cherry blossom carpets the outfield like a late snowfall.

The first calls of the cuckoo, usually at the beginning of the month, can be relied upon to lift the spirits even during the toughest day of cricket and the truly fortunate, distracted boundary fielder might even catch the electric flash of a kingfisher plunging into the Pang. As the month progresses and temperatures rise, it is hard not to worry on behalf of the dogs and the youngest children who have been brought to watch the XI as soaring red kites take to the thermals and circle, bank, and glide along the valley.

Opening the batting on Pit at 11.30 on a Saturday morning has always been a challenge: the new ball will swing and seam extravagantly; however, by lunch, it becomes a much more straightforward proposition, and it has always been a pleasure to watch the future stars of the game playing for, and against, Bradfield on this glorious ground.

**Mr M. Hill, Master in Charge of Cricket, on Pit**

May Madrigals usher in the new month atop the chapel tower. It comes with the promise of summer warmth, mown pitches, and, one hopes, uncancelled cricket fixtures. All being well, the sound of leather on willow punctuates the afternoons as the tossing of cricket sweaters over boundaries adorns the pitches.

By May, the students are well into the cricket term. Sketches such as the above, drawn around 1880, remind us how timeless the game is at Bradfield. As one can see, its popularity predates Big School and the chapel.

Cricket has existed for centuries, but one thing has not changed: here is Major being mowed incessantly, an act that is no less a ritual of devotion to many a contemporary groundsman. Pit was not excavated until 1927, and thus Major serves here as the first team pitch.

MAY

And this precious work of the groundsmen is certainly not time wasted. The College looks extraordinary at this time of year.

Can one believe that the M4 was originally meant to run straight through the heart of the College and gouge across its pitches? Landowners of local import saved the College from such a fate.

Max, Major, Pit, Rectory, Hill 2, and New Ground have all received their striations.

Pit's legendary status in well known in cricketing circles. It was created from an old chalk quarry in 1927 and remains one of the country's most beautiful grounds. England legend Ted Dexter ranked it the third best pitch in England (behind Lord's).

Tradition tells that a 15-year-old Sachin Tendulkar once cleared the River Pang in one leap.

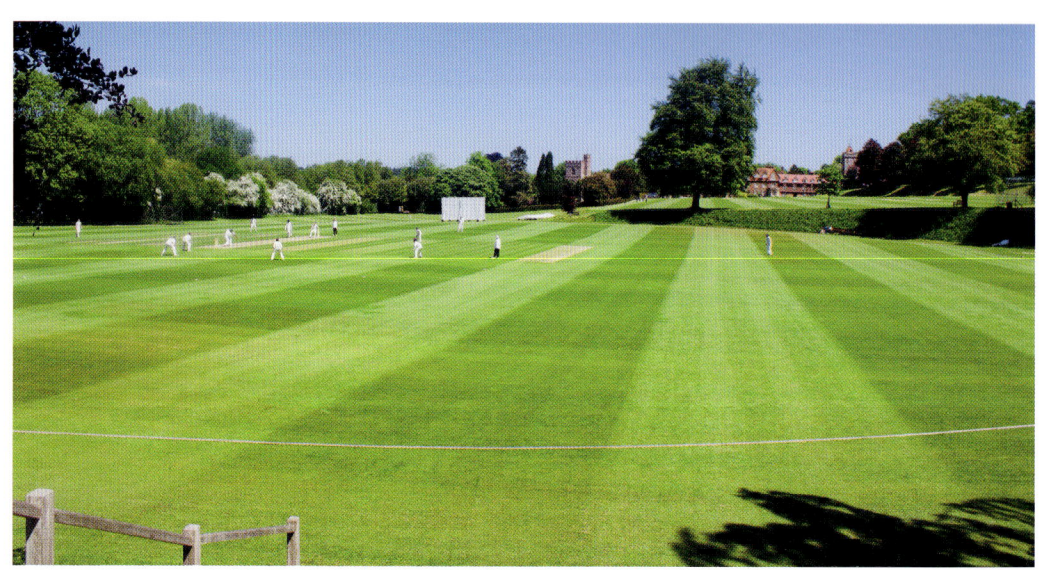

MAY

The eagle-eyed will note the old analogue scoreboard in the background of Pit.

The team negotiate a unique boundary on Major; Victorian earthworks render it a shape unknown to mathematics.

Hill 2 witnesses a Bradfield 'Six', and is well accustomed to it.

MAY

And what could top this achievement by the girls' 1st XI, playing at Lord's in the T20 final? This is a tournament that the Bradfield girls have won in the past, and where they always do the College proud.

The flag of St Andrew flies above Lord's.

MAY

The College's first ever cricket match was in 1852 against Magdalen College School, but the first match featuring just boys was against Radley in 1853. The first cricket professional was hired in 1859.

The quintessential appearance of a cricket team is not much changed, even over 150 years ago. However, the games programme has changed substantially. Today, over 600 students will be involved in a fixture on Saturdays, and several afternoons and evenings across the week will be dedicated to training. Even the financing has changed: up until the 1980s boys had to pay their own bus fare for away matches!

The 1st XI in 1858.

The warming season at Bradfield must have once been marked by a sharp decrease in trepidation when approaching 'Outers', the old Bradfield pool on New Ground. Despite being the descendant of heated indoor swimming baths (called 'Inners', built in 1867 at the back of the Quad), Outers was dug in 1898. It is separated from its successor by a slithering Pang.

That new pool was also outside, although a little more humane this time. Note the Old Gym in the background.

Its palimpsest, the current pool, is mercifully modern.

MAY

The summer term has a variety of other sports on offer besides cricket, and always has. Observe the conditioning of the boys by various means.

MAY

Not that this rigorous programme was merely for its own sake: see here the boys trained in hand-to-hand combat. Amongst the chief aims of the physical curriculum was to ready the boys for a world where, for many, war was a certainty. Indeed, warfare and service to the Empire was viewed by some as a public schoolboy's duty. British theatres of war have spanned the globe since the College's inception, from southern Africa up to northern Europe, from Central America around to Afghanistan (and there, three times, no less). Many Bradfieldians would go on to serve in the administration of the Empire and in the ranks of her armies, making self-defence an essential skill. Here, a master teaches basic grips and throws. One wonders how he selected his volunteers…

Bradfield is also known for its thriving athletics provision, and its reputation is historic. Note the lack of chapel tower in the following photographs, which helps date them to the very early 20th century at the latest.

MAY

MAY

MAY

As has been seen, the College is blessed with athletes, and our runners are especially impressive. The first records of cross-country events against other schools go back to 1920.

The highlight of the athletics calendar is, of course, Sports Day, where many of the events from the last 175 years are repeated. In 1918, Princess Alice presented the Sports Day awards.

MAY

Meanwhile, Bradfieldians excel in other sports throughout the year, from fencing to fives, swimming to sailing, tennis to riding. Whilst football, hockey, netball, and cricket are the preponderant sports, Bradfield excels at breadth.

As, of course, they always have done.

MAY

The 1917 1st XI football team.

The 1st VIII rowing team, 1933.

The 1934 fencing team.

MAY

Old Bradfieldian Football Club, Golfing Society, and Bradfield Waifs Dinner, 11th March 1932. The Waifs cricketers have recently won the national cup yet again.

And who could forget another great joy of the summer: the school day done, two pupils venture through the meadows for a round of golf.

# JUNE

## BOARDING AND HOUSE EVENTS

June is a special time of renewal and memory-making in the boarding Houses. As Leavers' Ball and a final Commem spent watching sport in the sunshine approach for the U6th, the next generation of JCR are appointed, the 6th Form induction week reunites the 5th Form, Faulkner's are increasingly integrated to Senior Houses, and the Year 7s and 8s strengthen links with Bradfield on visits. The Houses are busier at weekends with a revision focus and a recognition that social opportunities and 'Dells' are being enjoyed for the final time for some. House Outings, BBQs, U6th Dinners, warm evening walks, water parks, performances, packing, golf course, Greeker, summer fixtures and finals see the term build to an academic, social, and sporting crescendo until chapel clock strikes for the end of term. Calm descends; rest, recharge, farewells and then, the excitement of what the next year holds.

*Mr R. Penny, Deputy Head Pastoral*

June is here and the College is in full bloom. This photograph, taken from St Andrew's Church tower around 1900, shows the timeless charm of the summer months in the valley.

The view sweeps up Ashamptstead Road to Dark Lane, said by Bradfieldians to be haunted. Indeed, when boys used to arrive by train into Pangbourne, they would have to walk the unlit paths away from the Thames and into the stygian black of the valley. On those eerie nights, many a boy reported seeing a decapitated ghost roll its head down the hill and into the sleeping College.

The intriguing fact that Roman pottery kilns have been found on that hill was probably of little comfort to them.

As with all things at Bradfield, boarding is a charming concoction of the old and the new. Certainly, staff are far more involved in the evening provision than days of yore when prefects had dominion. For the tutors, getting to know the students outside of the classroom is one of the great pleasures of the job. Boarding ensures that all aspects of the young person can be developed by the College, and that every gifting, however quiet, can be nurtured.

House-on-the-Hill (D/G) was variously known as Modern Side or Naval Side (by distinction to Army Side) throughout its early years. It was created in 1899 with a view to accommodating boys who would go on to serve aboard Her Majesty's ships.

And as boarding grew, so did its needs. The quondam Continent Room was no longer able to house those who were 'not holding together', and thus a new 'san' was purchased. This then became Loyd House (A, right) and the 'san' was moved to what is now Stevens (K) House.

JUNE

It is fair to say that things were rather more spartan in times gone by. One could be forgiven for thinking this were some kind of hospital, but rather it is a dormitory in one of Bradfield's early houses. The curtained section is that of a prefect.

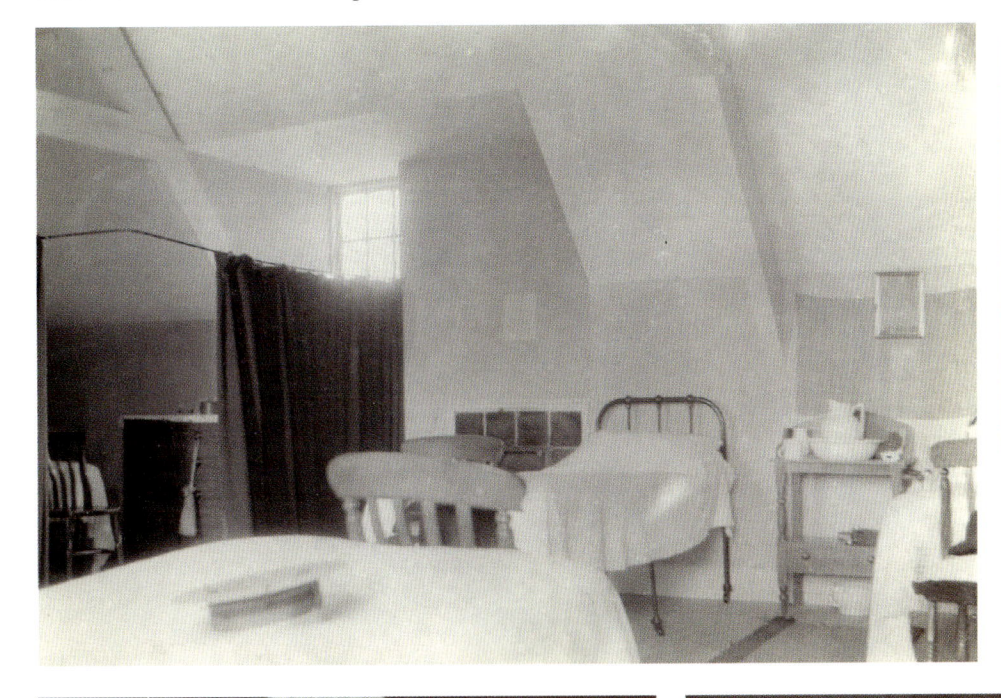

An A House junior dormitory in 1936. At this time, A House was located in the eastern portion of the Quad. Today, this is a geography classroom.

Tutors also needed accommodating and had simple rooms. It was not unusual for students to have permission to access some of these study areas and mull over a tome.

JUNE

Today, the spaces are far more generous-spirited. The rooms are welcoming, comfortable, and are open to a stamp of identity.

The communal areas are the perfect opportunity for students to mix, and for good advice to be passed down the year groups by the senior students. Houses become like families, and every family needs its living room.

The houses all have a variety of kitchens, called 'Brewers', for student use. The opportunity is there for the pupils to grow their culinary skills, although this author is yet to witness any in F House.

The housemasters and mistresses (Hsms) all have a study adjoining the house to their Private Side. Note the charming photo of the Greek Play on the wall of this housemaster's study.

These lockers were located in the classrooms and contained all the boy's worldly possessions. Called 'toys' rather than lockers, doing prep in the form rooms was thus charmingly called 'toy time'. Following a rather critical inspection (1960s), these were replaced with 'horseboxes', meaning desks with storage and a partition for pseudo-privacy.

The selection of photographs pinned on the toy door is an interesting window into what this student valued: his sports team, his family, and the setting of his College.

Grubs, the school tuck shop and site of pilgrimage for boarders, opened in 1896. Most recollections seem solely focused of the ice-cream produced by the shop's matron, which has become nothing short of mythical. The recipe has been lost, much to the despair of all.

JUNE

A unique aspect of Bradfield's provision is Faulkner's, a boarding house for the entire first year group. Here, pupils can mix with their year thoroughly before being separated into their senior houses, and allows for a more appropriate approach to the needs of 13-year-olds. It opened in 2000 for boys, being called West and East. The central elision between the two gables was added later to allow a greater integration of the two sides once girls were admitted.

Much weight is given to what one does for the house. Spanning the year, there are endless events where the houses do battle for trophies big and small, ensuring all have an opportunity to contribute and have their talents valued by their peers.

Staff and boys from several houses run the gruelling Tough Mudder.

House Darts can bring untold bragging rights.

Boys give it their all in House Hockey on the astro.

JUNE

House Dance is a real highlight. From some, the quality is extraordinary, and testament to real dedication. From others, the reliance on the sheer bafflement of overwhelming energy serves to entertain and bemuse in equal measure. Let's just say the boys do not often win… Of course, one can also attend the Dance Show, where the quality is professional.

JUNE

In House Golf, staff and students play alongside. Tutors seek not to disgrace themselves whilst the pupils vie for the hallowed cup. Win or lose, Bradfield's golf course, opened in 1998, is stunning.

House Harmony requires particular endeavour, and there is nowhere to hide. Yet, untrained and unsure singers still come together for the sake of the house and sing their hearts out.

B House hope for swift times in the House Obstacle Course.

House dinners are also keenly enjoyed; the students relish the opportunity to gather in the Dining Hall and sing to their families.

JUNE

It must be confessed that not all house events have quite the same dignity. Observe the house pancake and watermelon-eating competitions.

JUNE

Competitions fought and spoils won, these boys can now relax of an evening, employing complex rigging to improvise a cinema with a bedsheet outside their boarding house.

Hillside (F) old (1938) and new. WW2 pilot Hugh Percy is fourth from left, seated row.

Percy went on to study at St John's College, Cambridge, where he learned to fly with the University Air Squadron and was called to service soon after the outbreak of war. After converting to Defiants, a two-seater turret fighter, he was posted to 264 Squadron at Duxford on 19 June 1940 and fought in the Battle of Britain.

On 22 May 1944, four Spitfires from 610 Squadron took off to the Guernsey area on an armed shipping reconnaissance flight. The flight leader was 24-year-old Flt Lt Percy in a MkXIV Spitfire RB162.

During the German occupation of the Channel Islands, the German military had placed two anti-aircraft guns on the roof of Brehon Tower at Fort Brehon, near the tiny island of Herm. During the mission Percy was hit by anti-aircraft fire from the tower (similar to a Martello tower) on the east coast of Guernsey in the Little Russell channel; an area pilots often referred to as 'Flak Alley'.

At the time, he radioed to say, 'I've been hit. I'm climbing to gain height to bail out', which he did at 1,500 feet. Unfortunately, his parachute failed to open, and his aircraft crashed into the sea. Percy's body was never recovered.

June also hosts The Colour Run. The festival is so much more than the laughter and dust: it is an annual event which encourages students to consider the beauty in difference.

JUNE

Jazz on a Summer's Evening is another highlight of June. Students perform in Greeker beneath the stars, bringing their vibrant alchemy of improvisation and technique to a rapt audience.

JUNE

JUNE

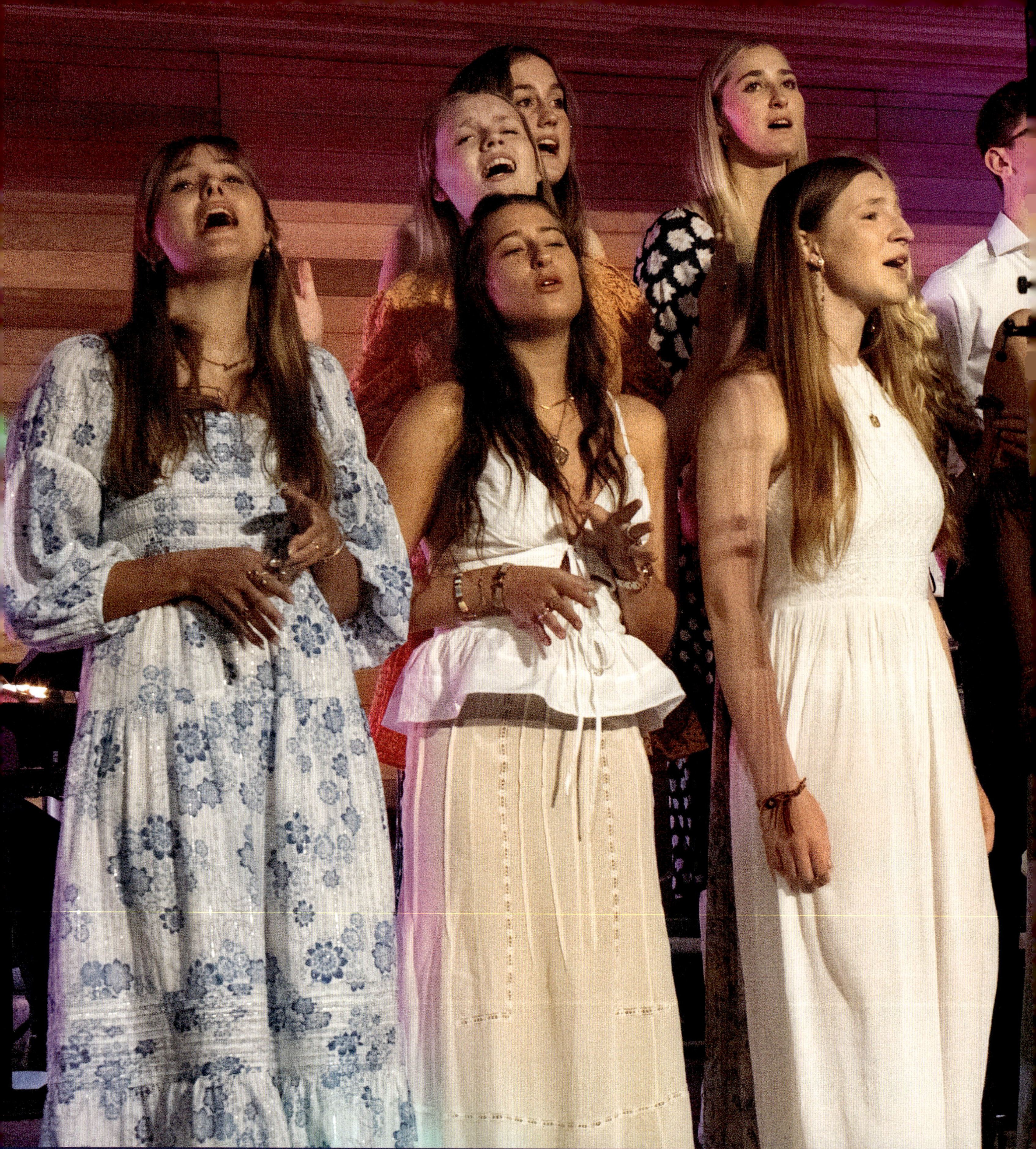

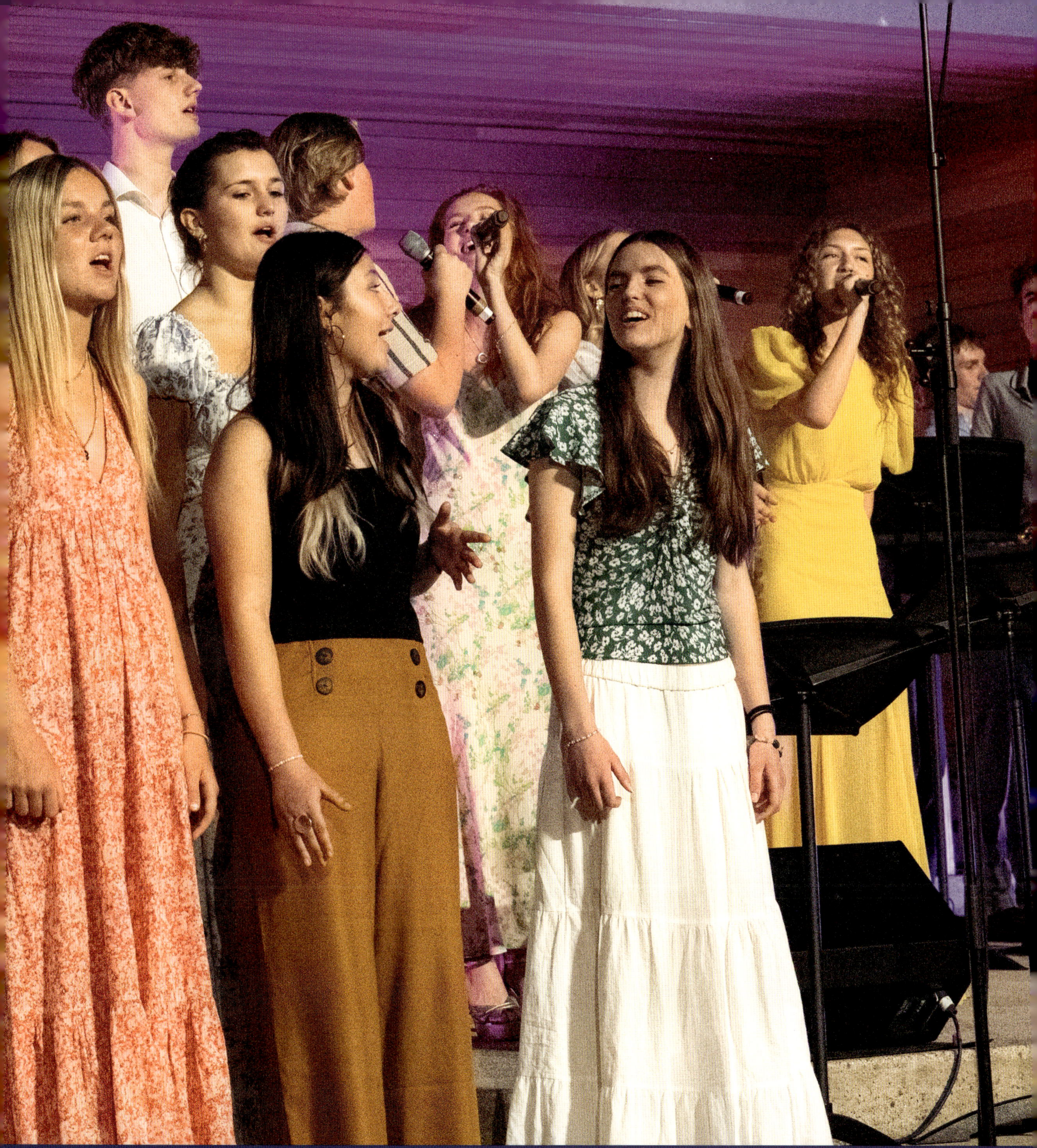

# JULY

## DRAMA

In the interest of being succinct when describing a month for which so much can be said, I would say the month of July is one of wonder, excitement, curiosity, and creativity – thus, it is as felicitous a time as any for theatre to be on full display at Bradfield. Summer-time productions are beautiful things here; students wishing to don their theatrical hats, and the audience before them, are able to vicariously experience pain, love, tension, fear, and so much more while a summer production is being performed, but, perhaps more importantly, and certainly more powerfully, passion is everywhere. The production of a summer play is an admirable and exciting experience, where students and staff collaborate to eclectically build something new and their own. Performances in July are not the only things to be enjoyed, however; the Greek plays – performed every three years – are a perfect example of this: their allegorical subtleties and cathartic features, mixed with tradition and entertainment, provide, I think, an excellent summary of this magical month – a month filled with passion, learning, appreciation, and entertainment.

**Jackson Frieda, current drama scholar**

The College is in all its glory, but also its final month. This 1884 watercolour captures how entwined the campus is with its surroundings at this time of year. The motion between wheat and brick feels seamless.

The 1884 view is now impossible to replicate, not least due to the amount of trees planted and nurtured since that century.

Drama is special at Bradfield, and not just because of its famous theatre. Drama is a chance to grow in confidence and creativity, but also an opportunity to 'be' someone else and thus explore your own identity. Therefore, the Faulkner's Play is a perfect opportunity to bind together a newly assembled year group and begin to cultivate those very skills. In this production, every single Faulkner's student performed.

JULY

Drama is also an opportunity to help the students and their audience to reflect on current and past events. Take this production of *Journey's End*, performed on Remembrance Sunday, or the performance of *Kindertransport*, a dramatisation of a woman's escape from Nazi Germany. Amazingly, one of the surviving *kinder*, Professor Leslie Brent, came to watch the performance and agreed to answer the pupils' questions. Professor Brent came to Britain on the very first train in 1938.

The recent Senior Play, *4.448 Psychosis*, was another such opportunity for art to shape life. This touching and brutal reflection on mental health inspired a broad spectrum of discussion, lessons, and reflection.

Some are surprised to know that the Greeker plays host to a number of non-Classical productions. Witness in these pages how the Greeker can be transformed to suit any tone or period, fitting seamlessly into the *Knight of the Burning Pestle*, 1954.

JULY

And here also, in this production of the *Merchant of Venice*, 1968. One could be forgiven in thinking this were a genuine Tudor theatre (and, dare I say, the Globe?)!

Of course, maintaining fidelity to the Hellenic was entirely appropriate when it came to this 1916 production of a *Midsummer Night's Dream*.

Hal and Hotspur do battle in 1948's *Henry IV, Part 1*. In vanquishing Hotspur, Hal not only proves his courage, but also symbolically conquers the old model of leadership, asserting his place as a future king who will blend honour with the political sagacity necessary to rule. This duel becomes the fulcrum upon which Hal's reputation and destiny pivot, marking his emergence as a worthy successor to the crown.

The leading cast of *Hamlet* in 1875, complete with ghost.

Hamlet woos Ophelia in 1969.

Justice befalls the false king.

JULY

Plays have also been performed in the chapel. *Murder in the Cathedral*, performed in 1966, is one such example.

And *Galileo* by Brecht.

And *Romeo and Juliet*.

Plays have even been performed in the Thai Garden, such as *Blood Wedding*.

JULY

But no matter where one performs, the costuming can often be what is most transportative. Typically designed and fashioned by members of the College, they always appear utterly effective.

*Hamlet* from 1969.

*Taming of the Shrew* from 1971.

Drama pupils posing mid-rehearsal.

Bradfield has produced many famous and fine actors of stage and screen. Remembered with particular affection is one of our most celebrated performers, Tony Hancock. He is here pictured in the 2nd XI, but war is soon to break out and he will enlist with the RAF.

# THE GREEK PLAY

As a theatre director, a vast majority of one's working life is spent chewing a pencil hunched over a script in a darkened studio. But there are a lucky few who get to rehearse in the great outdoors – Drew McOnie in leafy Regent's Park, Rebecca Thomas in the windswept Minack – and I can assure you they are looked on with envy. Fortunately for the Head of Drama at Bradfield, the Greek Theatre allows membership of that elite club, and I cannot overstate what a privilege it is. Watching a pupil heroically stride through the skene doors to address the citizens of Thebes as the sun slowly sets in the distance and a muntjac softly barks from within the woodland: it is very hard to capture how special that is. When one considers were it not the intervention of its founder's wife, Greeker could easily have become another tennis court, but seeing the potential of the chalk pit she convinced him to transport the wondrous Theatre of Epidaurus, albeit slightly scaled down, to leafy Berkshire. Since then, generations of Bradfield pupils have had the opportunity to perform on its sacred ground, and I use that word fully aware of its implications. Peter Brook famously wrote of the sacredness of a performance space and nowhere is that truer than Greeker and nowhere have I been more grateful to have worked.

**Nic Saunders, Head of Drama and Director of *Oedipus* 2023**

After the rediscovery of the Great Theatre at Epidaurus in 1879, Frank Benson's 1880 Oxford production of *Agamemnon* inspired the headmaster and warden of Bradfield College, Dr Herbert Gray, to stage a production of Euripides' *Alcestis* in the College's Dining Hall (1882). Described as 'a plucky experiment' by the *Spectator* magazine, this first Bradfield Greek Play was followed by a production of Sophocles' *Ajax* at the University of Cambridge. Thus began what became the regular triennial of Oxford-Bradfield-Cambridge Greek Plays.

The Bradfield College History recounts how in 1888 the imaginative warden 'conceived the idea of converting [a chalk pit] into a Greek theatre, on the model of those existing in the best times of the Attic drama. With the aid of the boys, and afterwards with the help of professional workmen, he cut into the solid chalk ten tiers of seats, while he shaped the orchestra on the model of that at Epidaurus, in the Peloponnese – i.e. a complete circle or proper dancing place, such as existed when the Attic drama was little more than a series of hymns to Dionysus, interspersed with a monologue or dialogue between actors, from a temporary platform, introduced to give breathing time to the chorus… In June, 1890, Bradfield College, thus furnished, produced under unique conditions its first open-air Greek Play, the *Antigone* of Sophocles. "For the first time", said the journals of that date, "since the downfall of the Greek stage a Greek drama has been produced under conditions exactly identical with those of ancient times … in an open-air theatre, the proportions and acoustic properties of which Pericles might have envied."'

After the success of the *Agamemnon* of Aeschylus in 1882, the College put on *Alcestis*, followed by *Antigone*, followed by *Agamemnon*, at more or less regular intervals, which became the familiar three-year cycle for the playwrights (though, after 1928, not for the plays) of Euripides-Sophocles-Aeschylus.

Over the years, the fame of the Bradfield Greek Play spread far and wide. Prime Ministers, poets, generals, archbishops, writers and actors have all supported this unique event. T.S. Eliot, Sybil Thorndyke, Agatha Christie, Lord Asquith, Field Marshal Lord Montgomery, Sir Peter Hall, and Enoch Powell were all faithful pilgrims.

> THE ONLY SAD THING ABOUT THE BRADFIELD PLAY IS THAT WHEN WATCHING ONE, ONE KNOWS IT WILL BE THREE YEARS BEFORE ONE CAN SEE ANYTHING SO GOOD ANYWHERE IN ENGLAND.
>
> **1928: John Masefield, poet laureate 1930–1967**

Sketch from 1895.

THE GREEK PLAY

THERE ARE SURELY FEW AMONG THOSE WHO COME TO SEE AND HEAR A GREEK PLAY AT BRADFIELD WHO DO NOT GO AWAY FEELING BETTER, BROADER AND BIGGER-SOULED.

**Dr Herbert Gray, former headmaster (1922)**

The Greeker, now the College's crown jewel, has the most humble of origins. In the middle of the 1800s it was a chalk pit, a far cry from the national renown of today.

The notion of an obdurate Gray collaring a few hearty boys to come and dig a Greek theatre is alien to us today, but dig it they did!

The Greek Play would be announced by a trumpeter marching through the village, tooting away whilst a crier in classical attire would cry out in ancient Greek. Once assembled, the trumpeter would announce the entrance of the headmaster, to whom he would bow, and the audience would rise. Choral sticks would strike the ground in unison, and the play could begin.

As arcane as this may sound the practice endured until very recently, and many current staff recall it well.

Eager arrivals in 1900 on either side of the archway. The Greek Play was advertised in major cities around Europe and America; posters were put up in French train stations and reviews in New York newspapers.

THE GREEK PLAY

The Greek Plays have ever been spectacles. In this 1928 production of *Rhesus*, the bursar very kindly lent the boys his horses upon hearing that their chariot was bereft. One marvels that the horses played their parts so well in such a crowded space, and thus at the skills of the young charioteer.

> I have been more consistently happy in Greeker than anywhere else at all
>
> **Richard Adams (H 33–38), author of *Watership Down***

THE GREEK PLAY

See here the 1892 production of *Agamemnon*, the first play in Aeschylus' *Oresteia* trilogy. After 10 years of war, Agamemnon returns, charioted to Mycenae beneath a clouded victory, his homecoming undercut by songs of tragedy.

The chorus, having yearned for the end of the war, is now filled with unease, murmuring through the palace that victory must be paid for.

Queen Clytemnestra welcomes Agamemnon with outflung devotion, but longs to murder him within her heart. He sacrificed their daughter, Iphigenia, and thus his return opens a wound that festers beneath the scene.

The crimson tapestries she spreads before him, ostensibly in honour of his victory, are rich with symbolism, causing the king to walk upon both blood and hubris. Fate feels inescapable in this scene, and justice draws slowly in like an evening shadow.

THE GREEK PLAY

The same scene plays out in the 1949 production. Cassandra, the doomed prophetess taken from Troy, follows her captor into this foreign land. She has perfect sight of the future, but is cursed with words none shall believe.

The leader of the chorus mourns the beauty of Helen and the coming downfall of the palace.

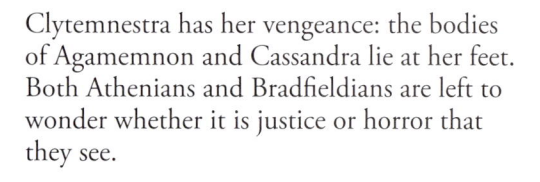

Clytemnestra has her vengeance: the bodies of Agamemnon and Cassandra lie at her feet. Both Athenians and Bradfieldians are left to wonder whether it is justice or horror that they see.

THE GREEK PLAY

The murderess now stands triumphant in 1976. 33 years stand between these productions, yet the hollow eyes of the chorus still leer in judgement and eternal witness.

THE GREEK PLAY

*Alcestis* in 1914. Admetus greets Heracles, who wears a fox fur in lieu of a lion. In the 1895 production of *Alcestis*, Admetus was played by Headmaster Gray (below).

The grandeur of the funeral procession.

THE GREEK PLAY

Behind the scenes, boys have their costumes readied on the Hillside Rux (1914).

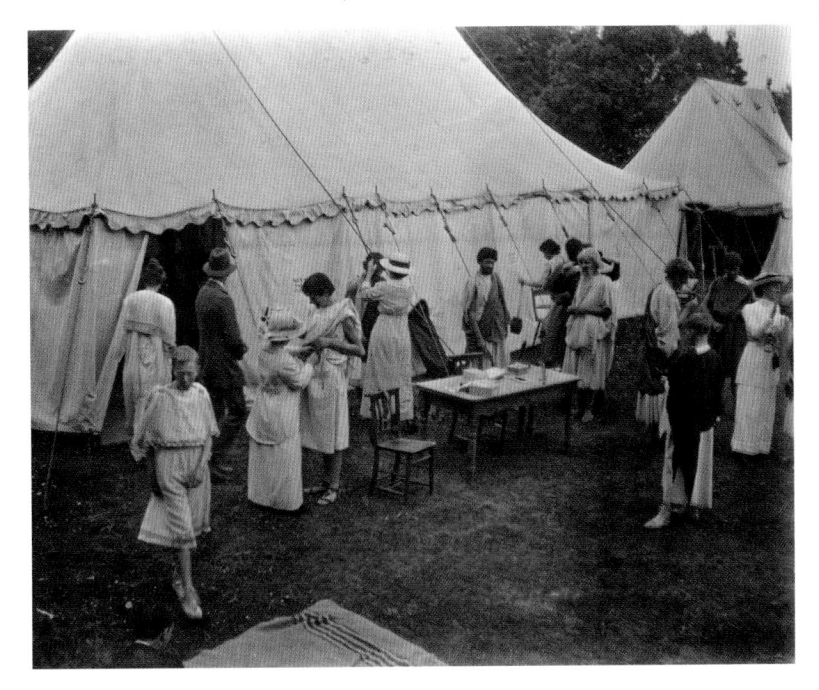

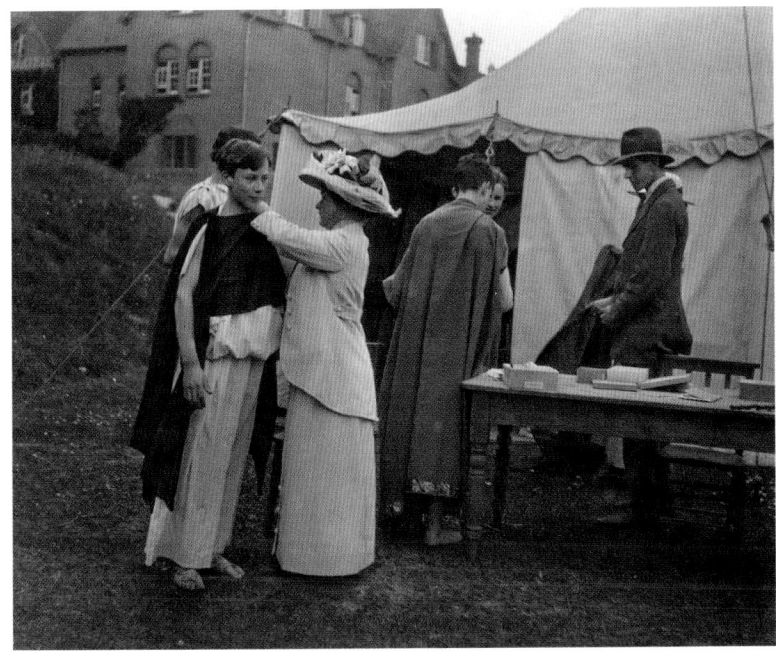

Guests arrive by motorbus and horse-drawn carriage.

THE GREEK PLAY

233

Eurydice is mourned in *Antigone*, 1890.

The blind prophet, Tiresias, is led by his guide. In *Antigone*, he speaks the words of the gods, and of the Fate all are beholden to. By prophesying the consequences of immorality to the king, he does so also to the Athenian audience.

Here, Tiresias gives his same fatal warnings, although now it is 1922.

Having not heeded the soothsayer, the gods take King Creon's son, Haemon. He lifts supplicant's hands, but Fate has woven on.

THE GREEK PLAY

Miss Butler

# THE ALCESTIS
## OF
## EURIPIDES.

THE OXFORD TEXT

WITH

ENGLISH VERSE TRANSLATION

BY

SIXTH FORM BOYS

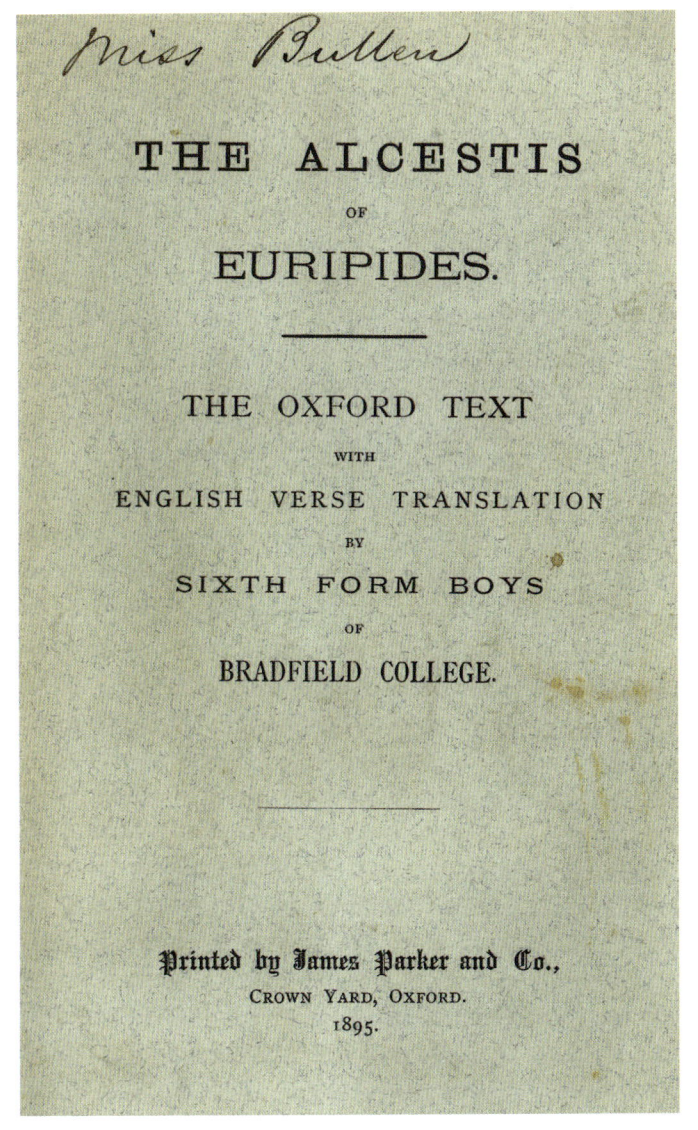

OF

BRADFIELD COLLEGE.

Printed by James Parker and Co.,
Crown Yard, Oxford.
1895.

The Greek Play has had a central place at the College for almost 150 years. The effort the Sixth Form put into this *Alcestis* translation in 1895 shows the care they took even in those early days.

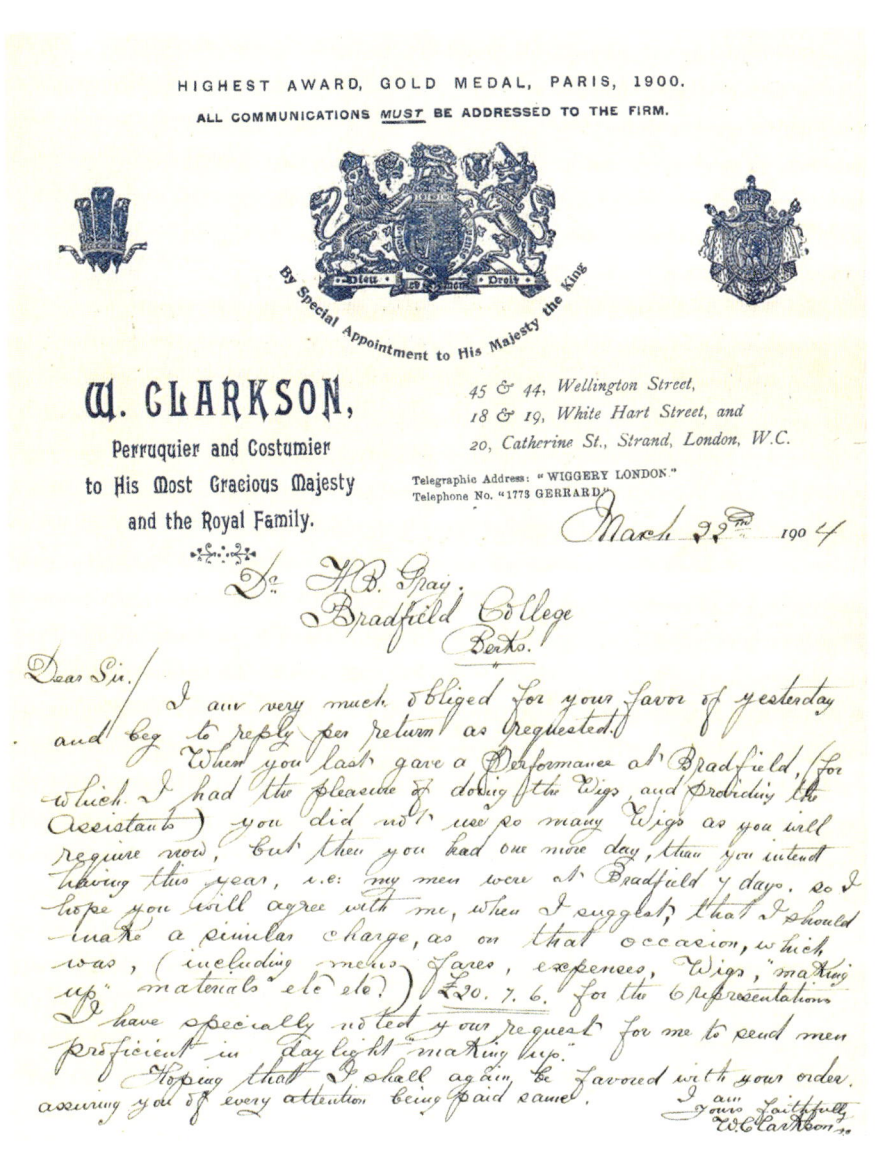

Wigs were made specially at the London Wiggery on The Strand. In this 1904 letter, W. Clarkson gives one an insight into this long-lost form of communication.

**THE GREEK PLAY**

## ORDINARY LOCAL TRAIN SERVICE

| READING | dep. | 12.49 p.m. | | |
|---|---|---|---|---|
| THEALE | arr. | 1.3 p.m. | | |
| NEWBURY | dep. | *12.50 p.m. | 2.3 p.m. | |
| THEALE | arr. | *1.12 p.m. | 2.25 p.m. | |
| | | | | |
| THEALE | dep. | 5.36 p.m. | 7.4 p.m. | |
| READING | arr. | 5.47 p.m. | 7.18 p.m. | |
| THEALE | dep. | 5.42 p.m. | 6.20 p.m. | 7.5 p.m. |
| NEWBURY | arr. | 6.4 p.m. | 6.43 p.m. | 7.27 p.m. |

*Saturdays only, but see below for special arrangements for a train leaving Newbury for Theale at 1.37 p.m.*

## SPECIAL ARRANGEMENTS

*ARRIVAL*

A train leaving PADDINGTON at 12.30 p.m. will call specially at THEALE at 1.25 p.m. Luncheon-car. Cheap day tickets will be available to passengers travelling from Paddington to Theale and back as follows: First Class, 8s. 0d. return; Third Class, 5s. 3d. return.

The 11.22 a.m. train from Bristol to Paddington (Newbury 1.37 p.m.) will call specially at Theale to set down passengers.

*DEPARTURE*
Depart THEALE.

6.45 p.m. Train for Newbury, Trowbridge, Westbury, and the Weymouth line, connecting at Newbury with the 7.18 p.m. train for the Winchester and Southampton line, and at Westbury with the 8.14 p.m. train for Bath and Bristol (Stapleton Road).

7.15 p.m. Train for READING and PADDINGTON. Dining-car.

## CONNECTIONS AT READING

Depart READING.

6.6 p.m. For Bath, Bristol, Weston-super-Mare.
6.49 p.m. For Oxford, Worcester, Malvern.
7.18 p.m. For Cheltenham, Bath and Bristol.
7.47 p.m. For Oxford.
8.25 p.m. For Oxford, Worcester and Malvern.
8.40 p.m. For Bristol and Weston-super-Mare (slip carriage).

---

The Greek Play was an international event, as well as a national one. Special train arrangements were even required, as here in 1937, to allow for such an occasion.

The accompanying invitation shows the hurdles, old and new, that must be leaped to ensure a successful performance.

One programme from the early 20th century records thanks to an African king for donating a lion skin to help make the production more authentic.

---

THE HEADMASTER OF BRADFIELD COLLEGE

*Requests the Honour of the Company of Yourself and Friends*

on Saturday, June 19th, or Tuesday, June 22nd,
or Thursday, June 24th, or Saturday, June 26th, 1937,

*to witness the performance of*

THE 'OEDIPUS TYRANNUS' OF SOPHOCLES

*in the Greek Theatre.*

---

THE PLAY will begin punctually at 3 p.m. The gates of the Theatre will not be opened until 2.25 p.m. and will be closed at 2.55 p.m. *No admission is possible afterwards, since the approaches to the Auditorium are from below only, and late-comers would therefore interfere with the action of the Players. For the same reason it is not possible to leave the Theatre before the end of the performance.* A Herald with a Trumpet will announce the beginning of the Play.

Visitors are asked kindly not to use sunshades or umbrellas, which would obstruct the view of others. Tea will be provided at a moderate charge, immediately after the Play.

TRAINS AND CONVEYANCES. On each of the days of the Play the 12.30 p.m. train from Paddington will stop specially at Theale at 1.25 p.m., and in the evenings a train will stop specially at Theale at 7.15 p.m. and will arrive at Paddington at 8.10 p.m. Particulars of these trains and of other special arrangements and of the ordinary service of trains between Theale and Reading and Newbury will be found on the back of this invitation.

Omnibuses will meet these trains and will take visitors back to Theale after the Play.

INVITED GUESTS are requested to fill in the attached form and send it *before May 1st* to *The Hon. Secretary, Greek Play Committee, Bradfield College, Berks.* Tickets of admission will be sent out about May 15th.

THE HON. SECRETARY will be saved much correspondence *if* (1) *one definite day is fixed upon in answering this invitation*; (2) *an alternative day is suggested, if convenient*; (3) *answers of acceptance are confined to this sheet.*

BRADFIELD COLLEGE,
February 1937.

---

## TICKETS

To THE HON. SECRETARY, GREEK PLAY COMMITTEE, *Bradfield College, Berks.*

Day and Date for which Tickets are required ................

*Alternative date, if convenient* ................

Number of Tickets required. (*Write number in figures. Not more than 4 tickets can be issued on one invitation form*)

Name (*in block capitals*) ................

Address (*in block capitals*) ................

Date of Signature ................

Whilst it is one thing to learn Classical Greek, it is quite another to sing it. Choral odes were typically composed in strophic pairs (strophe and antistrophe), with matching metrical patterns, and an epode with a different meter. Colometry (the practice of dividing lines of poetry into 'cola' ((smaller rhythmic units)) to guide the singers in their delivery) must also be negotiated. Now add in that Classical Greek is sung in a qualitative meter, a meter based on the length of syllables (mora and morae) as opposed to stresses. A long syllable typically has twice the duration of a short syllable. And this is to say nothing of the requisite microtonality, relative pitch, antiphonal style, and the distinction between modes, such as Phrygian or Lydian.

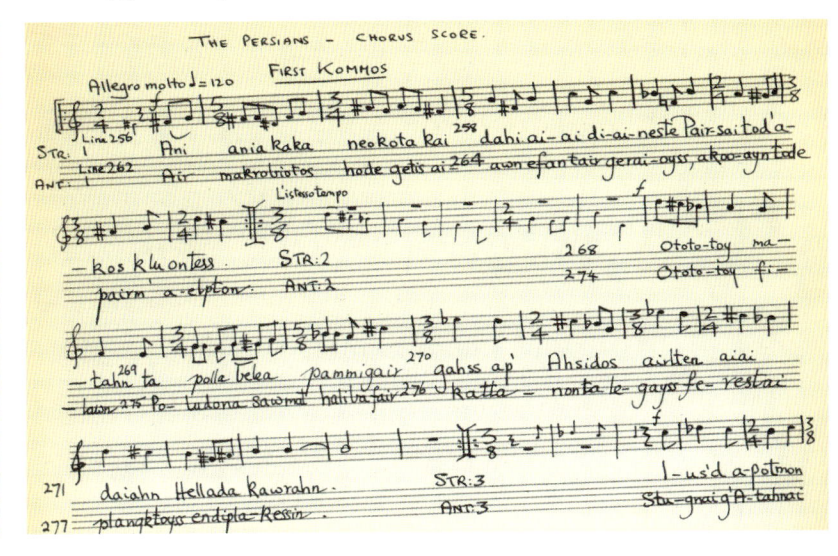

Then, of course, comes the dancing. These sheets, taken from a performance of the *Persians*, remind us of such challenges.

THE GREEK PLAY

After a brief interlude where the Greeker became impracticable, a 2011 campaign was launched to restore Greeker to its former glory and the refurbished Greek Theatre re-opened in May 2014.

To celebrate the re-opening of the theatre, Bradfield held a Gala Performance on 10 May 2014. The event was hosted by Old Bradfieldians Mark Nicholas (television presenter), Claudia Harrison (actress) and Jonny Saunders (radio presenter and housemaster), and included performances from pupils, past and present.

John Etheridge performs at the reopening.

PERFORMING IN THE GREEK THEATRE LED ME TO TRY THE PROFESSION FOR REAL. THE EXPERIENCE OF WORKING IN THAT SPACE HAS STAYED WITH ME AND ALWAYS WILL.

**Claudia Harrison, actor and Old Bradfieldian**

THE GREEK PLAY

As for the most recent Greek Play, that was a performance of *Oedipus Rex*. That legacy stretches back to 1937, as seen here.

THE GREEK PLAY

Although the efforts of the students are much lauded, one must not forget the efforts of countless generations of staff. One sees Cecil Bellamy, the producer of the 1937 production, at the very heart of the choreography and energy of the scene. The costumes, props, blocking, music, and set are outstanding.

*Oedipus* in 1979 was a graphic affair, but still had all the fidelity of the previous incarnations. Oedipus' blinding stands amongst the most harrowing acts of punishment in Greek tragedy, a moment laden with profound symbolic weight. His eyes, which had long been blind to the truth of his own existence, become, in his anguish, the instruments of his suffering. By plucking them out, Oedipus enacts a visceral form of atonement, for he can no longer bear to look upon the world, the people he has wronged, or the tragic reality of his own deeds. His blinding also signifies a deeper metaphysical shift: in destroying his vision, Oedipus transcends the physical realm and enters a state of 'inward seeing', removing the abstruse limits of human understanding and the crushing weight of Fate. It is both a punishment and a release, a way of severing his connection to the rebarbative world and embracing the darkness he believes he deserves. His eyes, once the instruments of ignorance, now serve as a conduit for his tragic enlightenment, a final act of desperate clarity in a play shaped by the inexorable forces of destiny.

THE GREEK PLAY

Here, the set is more labyrinthine, characterised by shadows and confusion. The bloody palate of stage and costume augments the themes of family, lust, danger, and mutilation.

THE GREEK PLAY

2023's *Oedipus* was the College's most recent Greek Play. Greek and English were blended for the first time, enabling a greater understanding and empathy for the story. After all, Athenian drama was devised to pose moral questions to a nascent democracy; those same challenges were posed two thousand years later in a way that all could understand.

THE GREEK PLAY

THE GREEK PLAY

The Greek Play is not just a pilgrimage site for classicists from around the world; the play itself travels. The 1979 *Oedipus* production, for instance, went to Cyprus, breathing that same Achaean air.

In the same tradition, the 2023 version toured to Greece, where it received the praise and appreciation of the Athenians. So much, in fact, that the Mayor of Alimos, Athens, awarded the cast the prestigious Medals of the Thucydidae for their services to Greek culture.

THE GREEK PLAY

THE GREEK PLAY

# AUGUST

## TRIPS AND FUTURES

A strange atmosphere exists amongst the departing Upper Sixth: a ubiquitous excitement for the future that lies ahead for all of us intertwined with the melancholy for what we leave behind as we depart Bradfield. We may all miss different aspects of Bradfield life; some may remember fierce matches on Rectory, others lessons with their favourite teachers, and many will reminisce about the time they spent with their friends in house. Yet all of our Bradfield experiences, however different they may have been, are alike in not only preparing us for, but shaping the very future that awaits us as Old Bradfieldians.

I shall always remember sitting in St Andrews for the last time before my final IB exam; though the sun was glaring through the windows, for a change, promising an exciting and bright summer ahead, I could not but feel overwhelmed by the melancholy of departing from this place that has meant so much to me.

**Georg Sparwasser, 2024 leaver, with offers from Cambridge and Harvard**

As another year draws to a close, one reflects and, in doing so, may dwell on the many years since the College's founding. This 1857 sketch of Rectory, with a possible Thomas Stevens (the Founder) in the foreground, points simultaneously to the change and consistency in the College's life.

AUGUST

The final note of the year comes in the form of 'Commem', a ceremony of celebration and tribute steeped in tradition. It begins with the Junior Common Room (the prefects) circling the Greeker's orchestra and striking sticks against the ground in unison.

The structure appears to have changed somewhat since 1899, but not the tone or purpose. The prize giving is particularly special, as Bradfield chooses to celebrate not just academic achievement, but also integrity, conduct, and kindness.

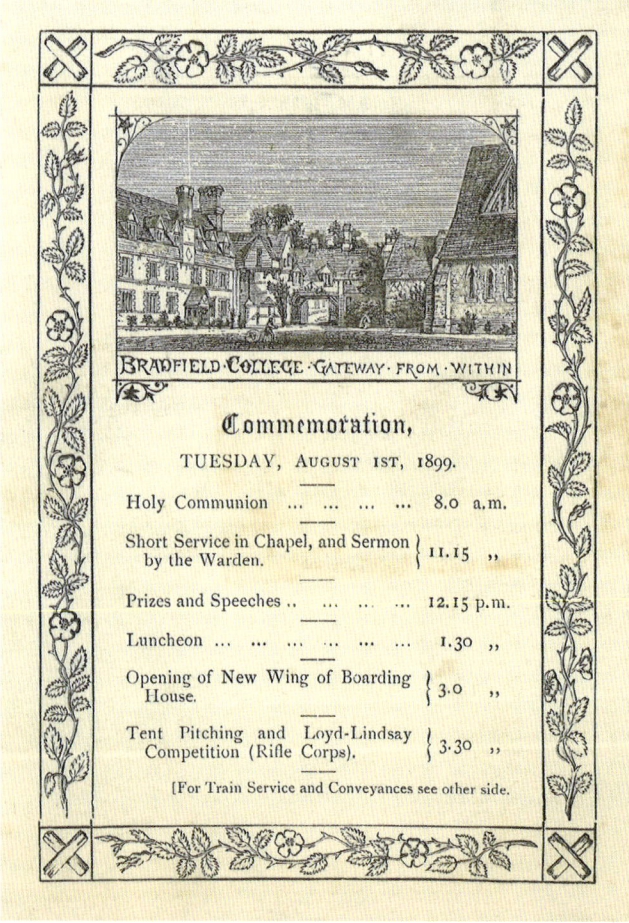

The headmaster descends into the orchestra to deliver his address.

But August is most keenly felt by one year group: our leavers. For them, it is their first August in 14 years where they are no longer bound to a school. For some time now their eyes have been turned to the future and the promise that it holds. Pictured here are photographs from those final months at the College, complete with networking events, careers fairs, and employer showcases. The jobs market has undergone a radical shift since 1850, yet the alchemy of excitement and trepidation has not left that final summer. The College can equip them, but also reassure them that their journey with the school is not over.

Indeed, for each year group the end of the year is different. For many, it means public or internal exams, but for the Faulkner's it is for adventure and adversity. They spend a week camping and hiking in the mountains of Wales only to return to high ropes, water sports, and mud runs. The challenges are immense, but the smiles tell the full story.

AUGUST

The Faulkner's are pit against the Brecon Beacons.

AUGUST

The Leavers' Ball brings the last weekend to an end. In the bittersweet of departures, it is always important to rejoice: after all, one is mindful of all that they have achieved, learned, created, and grasped. No matter what the future holds, they will carry Bradfield with them.

But for most, the holidays are not the end at all. Rather, it might be an opportunity to travel with the school. In perhaps one of the most profound shifts since 1850, students can now tour the world with their teachers and gain from their expertise.

Whether hiking up glaciers in Ecuador, setting up camp in Ethiopia on Christmas Eve (see overleaf), or receiving a prophecy at Delphi, the College reaches out into all corners of the world.

AUGUST

AUGUST

And so just like that the year sets. No two students from 1850 to today have had quite the same experience, or leave with the same memories. But it is my hope that everyone found a home at Bradfield, and felt that, even in fleeting moments, they were genuinely celebrated. As we're fond of saying here, there is one Bradfield, but many Bradfieldians. You can learn from some of the best teachers I have known; declare ancient words in a Greek Play; perform mesmerising jazz before hundreds; learn to shoot with GB hopefuls; score the winner in a national final; discuss your own poetry into the evening; hear from world experts in any field; fight quietly in the background for the success of your house; write a play; travel the world; leave a Bradfieldian.

# ST ANDREW'S

The academic years at Bradfield roll by, punctuated by familiar annual moments and by the changing seasons. Footballers seek shade under the lone tree by NG4 during the September trials. With the approach of Armistice Day, the Canadian maples along Chapel Bank have shed their red leaves into florid carpets on windless days. The reflection of a December full moon sparkles in the Pang at Iron Bridge as an eerie mist descends on Pit. On the AWP a bitingly cold east wind pierces the thermal layers, but the hockey player is warmed by a fleeting February daydream of that match in Singapore. How many pupils have looked up from their katsu curry to notice that the April sunset has brought the Burne-Jones windows into technicolour life? On Major, a dashing batter caresses a cover drive to the boundary, whilst in the nearby St Andrew's study centre, exam revision is in full swing. A cooling zephyr wafts through the mesmerised Greek play audience as day turns to night. Another generation of pupils leaves behind the energy and mischief of their teenage Bradfield years, but this beautiful place will live long in their memories.

**Mr R. Keeley, master at the College for over 30 years**

Despite the changes, the consistencies are often the most rewarding. St Andrew's, newly unveiled as a learning space, has been there since the very beginning of the College. It was, after all, the explicit wish of the Founder to create a choir for his parish church. After 175 years, the towers, windows, arches, and beams have circled their way back into the College.

St Andrew's was last restored by the Founder, Thomas Stevens, in 1848. However, the tower is Tudor and largely original.

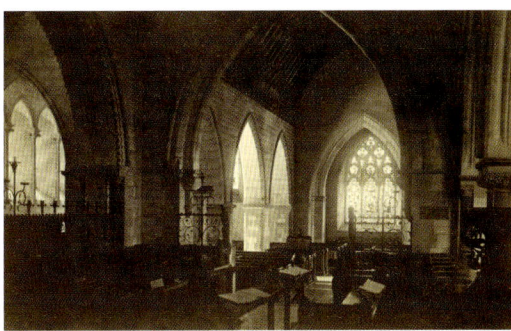

Once the chapel was built, the College had less need to use the parish church. However, keen to keep the connection, matins and major services were still held here across the year.

Keen to strengthen the connection further, Headmaster Roberts suggested that there be early morning prayers at the Founder's tomb. When that was discovered to be many feet beneath the ground, it was declared that the Founder's uncle's tomb would have to suffice.

The conversion was an extraordinary undertaking. Yet, despite the myriad complications and challenges, every effort was made to include the staff and students in the process. Pictured here, a pupil is taken through the construction and granted an awareness of the process.

Perhaps the greatest challenge of all was how to maintain, and even enhance, the beauty and idiosyncrasy of the building, much of which is medieval. I trust the reader would agree that those sensitivities were well placed and successfully delivered.

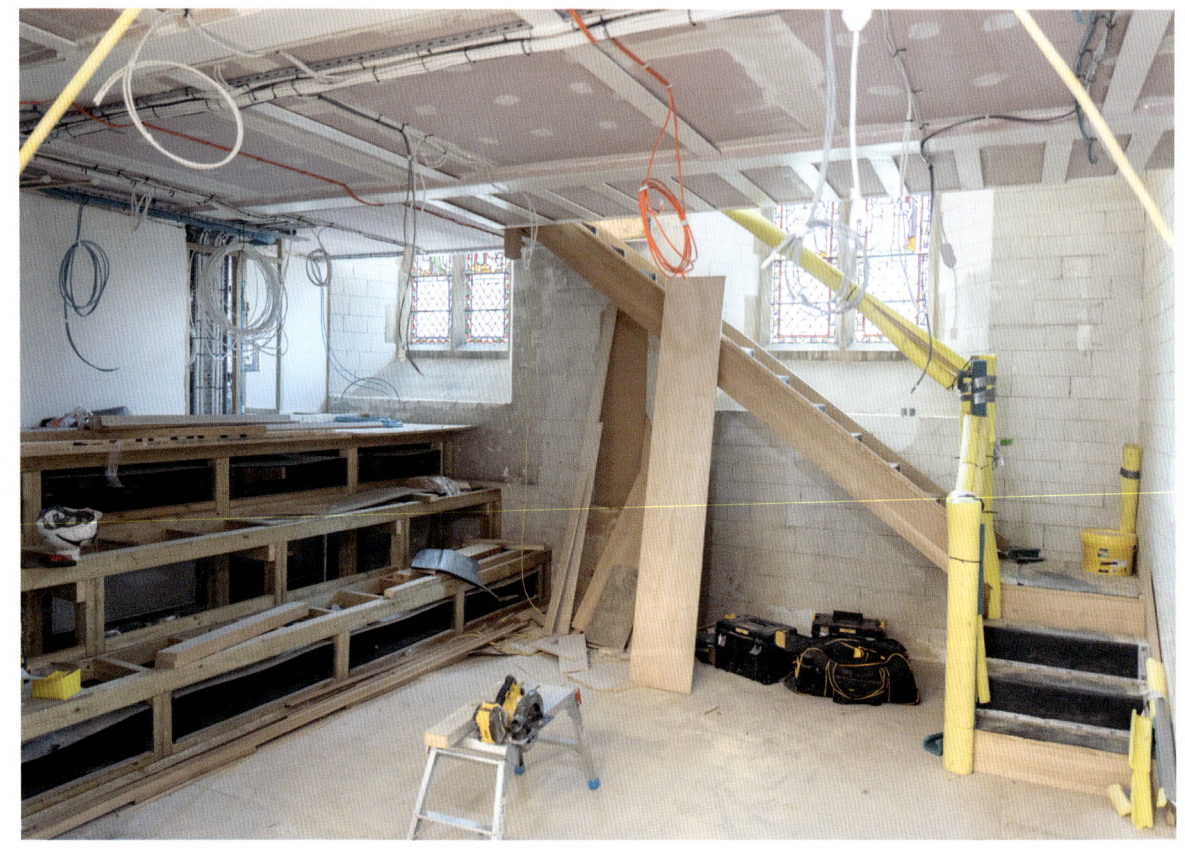

The intimate lecture theatre begins to take shape. Unusually for a deconsecrated church, it was not decreed that the font be removed or destroyed. It still stands proudly in place, and was where the Princess of Wales, Catherine Middleton, was christened.

After every success, the headmaster was delighted to receive the keys to this new exquisite and bespoke learning centre.

The entrance is now through a glass corridor which lets in soakings of light and neatly frames the restored Rose Window. The flowers and trees of the graveyard are to be appreciated on the approach.

ST ANDREW'S

Once inside, the space draws awe and sincerity. Each section has its intended purpose, as a seminar room, a lecture theatre, a reading room, a corner of quiet reflection, or an isolating pod for moments of redoubled focus. The space is a true marriage between productivity and atavism.

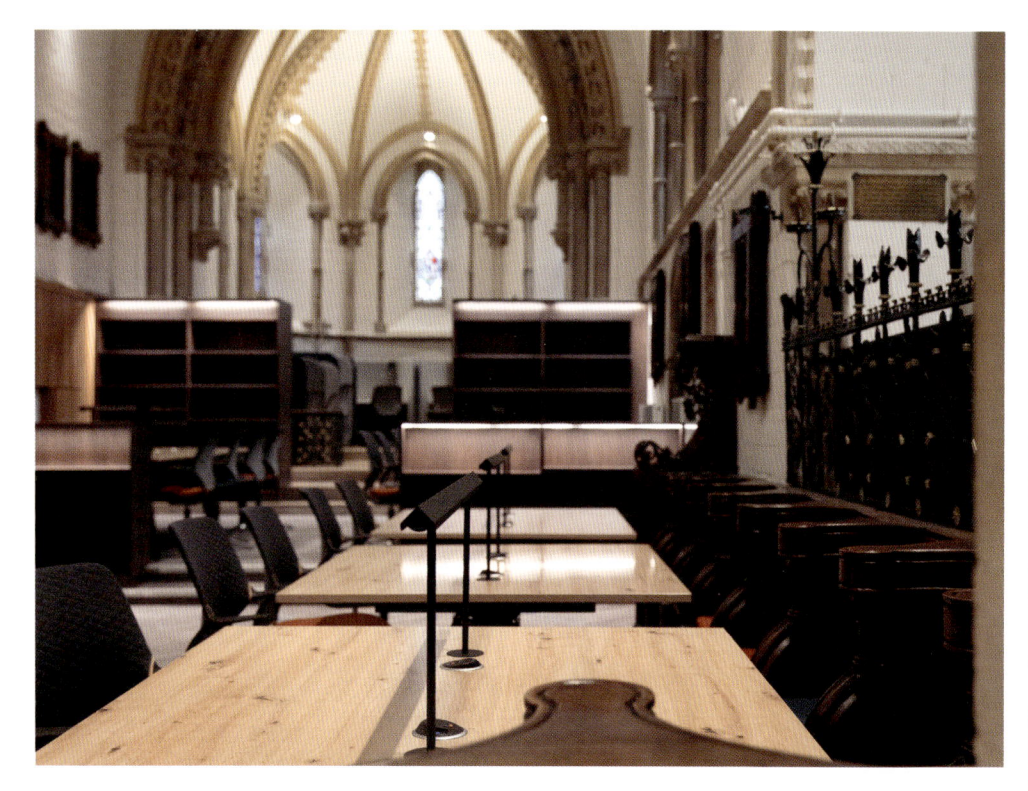

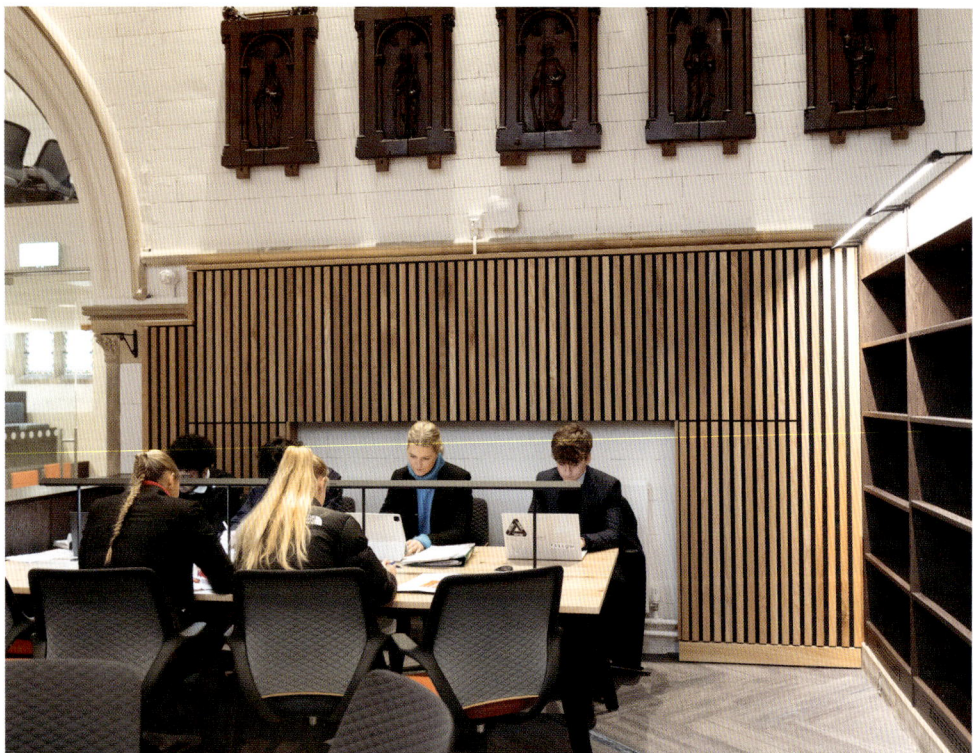

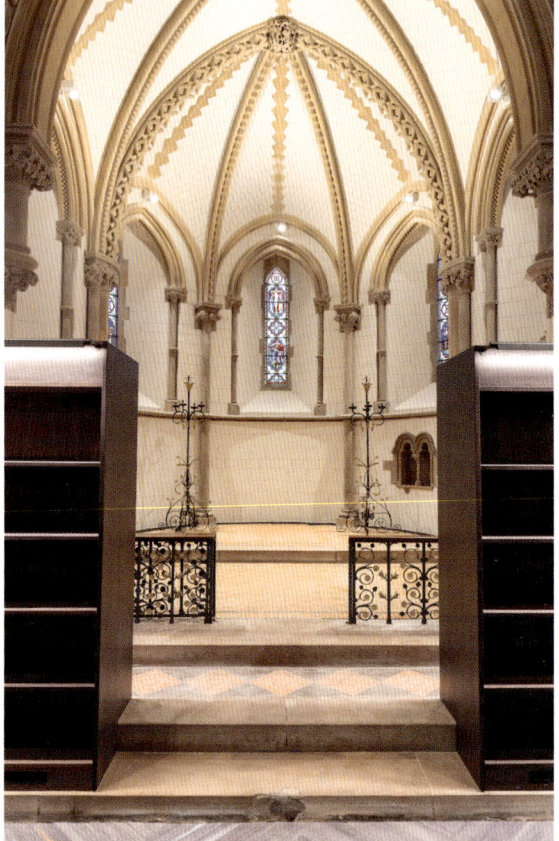

It must not be taken for granted that our students have what so many do not: the opportunity to work in beautiful spaces. Our buildings shape us and gives us access to the aesthetic, and to the virtues of order, pattern, shape, stability, and symmetry. The expectations of the students in this space comes so naturally to them; how could one fail to respect such a profound space?

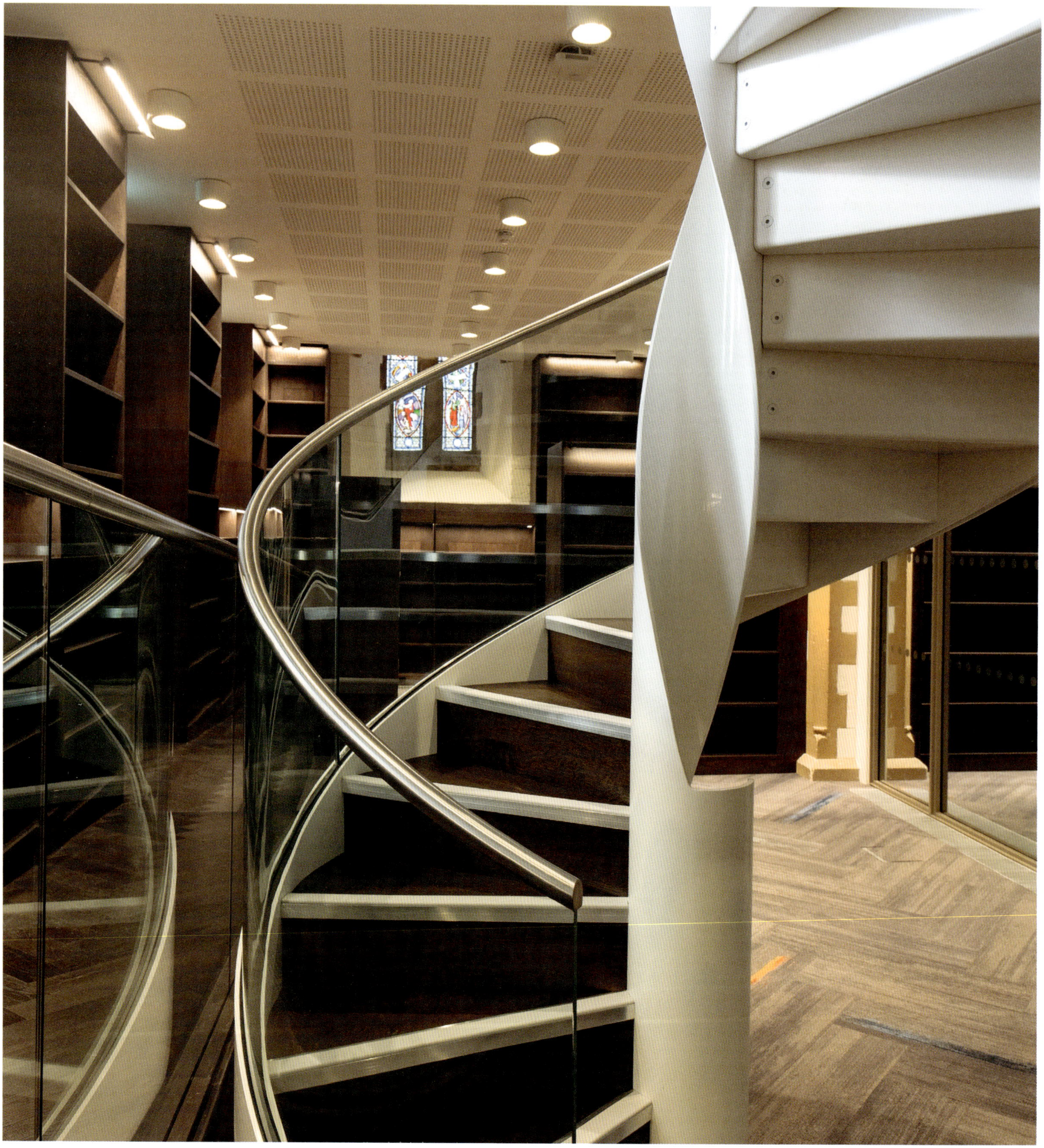

ST ANDREW'S

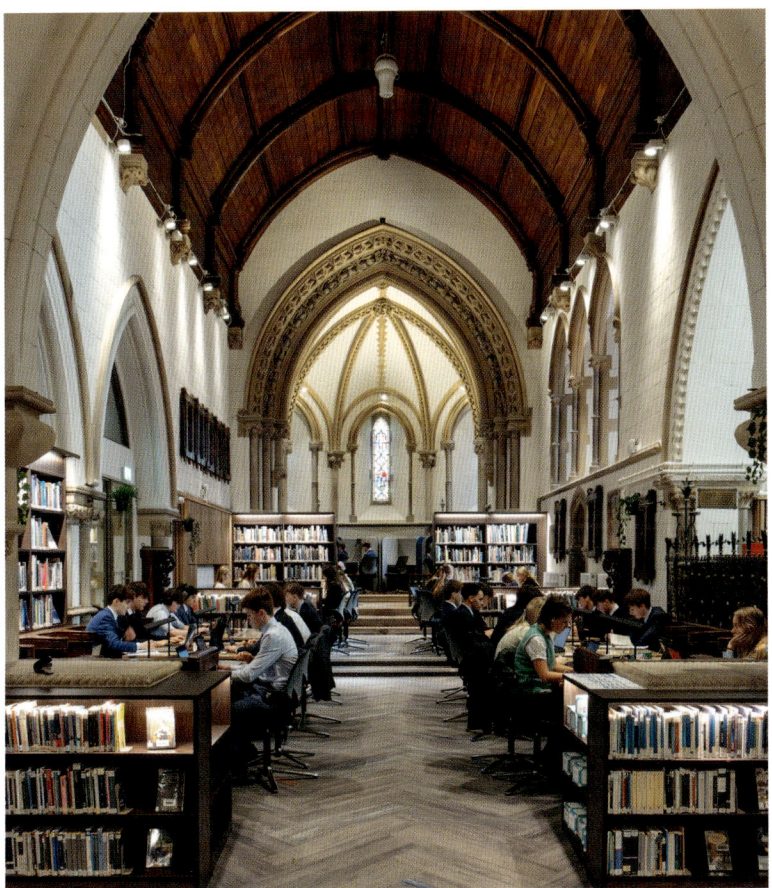

ST ANDREW'S

Bradfield College 2023–2024

ST ANDREW'S

Photo by Beaumont Photograph Group.

# AFTERWORD

175 years is a very notable milestone for any educational institution. It is a time to celebrate and be proud of everything achieved since the College's Foundation. Successful institutions like Bradfield preserve their best traditions whilst adapting to the changing conditions of their time. We should be confident that Bradfield will continue to walk this path and thereby thrive.

Those lucky enough to have enjoyed the opportunity of a Bradfield education will know the unique character of Bradfield and the beauty of its situation. So many Bradfield pupils over the years have made the most of the opportunities offered at Bradfield. They have developed as individuals and realised their potential. Importantly, they have gone on to make substantial contributions to society.

Bradfield has always been a charity. Today's Council continues to believe in Bradfield's charitable mission and its potential to benefit individual children and society. The Council is charged with overseeing the continuity of Bradfield's finest traditions whilst ensuring that Bradfield remains vibrant and relevant for current and future pupils in the years ahead.

**Tom Beardmore-Gray, Warden**

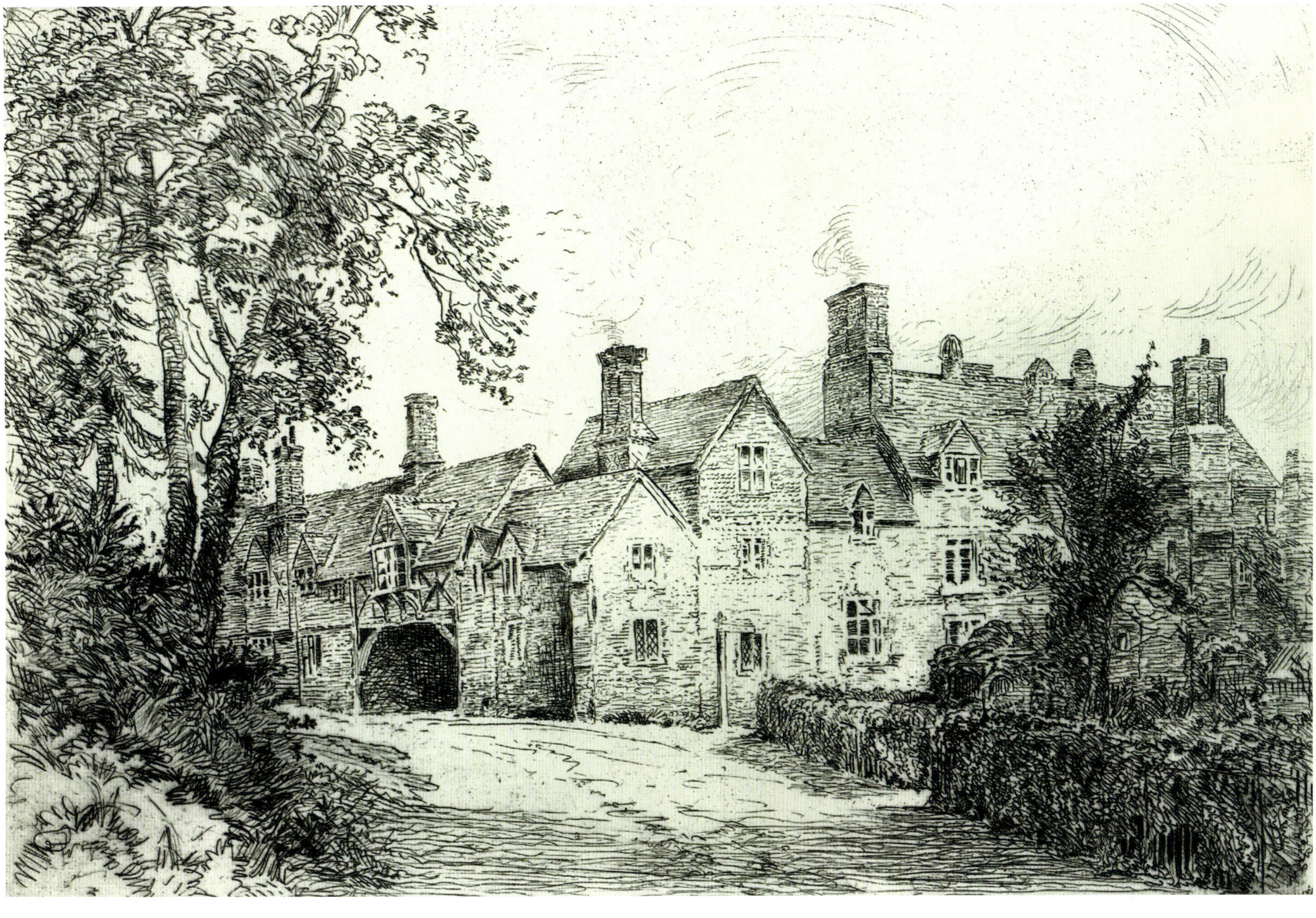

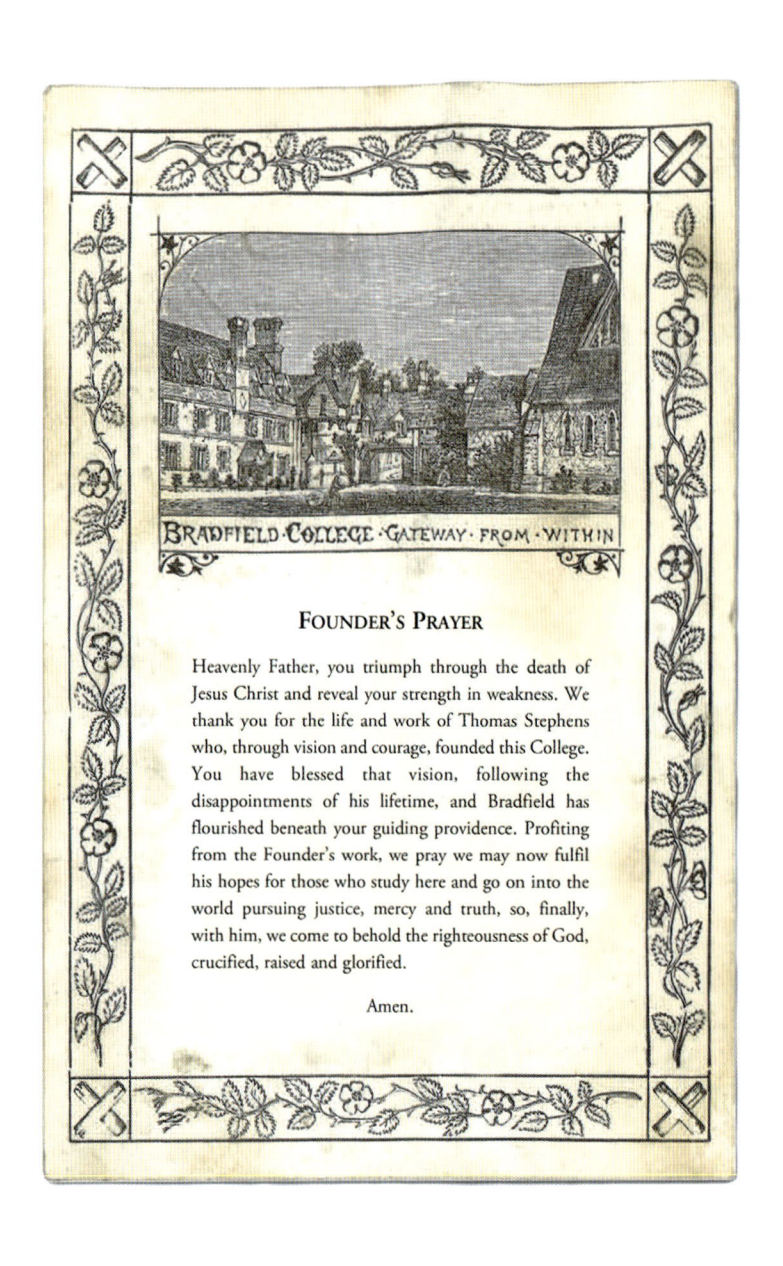

BRADFIELD COLLEGE · GATEWAY · FROM · WITHIN

### Founder's Prayer

Heavenly Father, you triumph through the death of Jesus Christ and reveal your strength in weakness. We thank you for the life and work of Thomas Stephens who, through vision and courage, founded this College. You have blessed that vision, following the disappointments of his lifetime, and Bradfield has flourished beneath your guiding providence. Profiting from the Founder's work, we pray we may now fulfil his hopes for those who study here and go on into the world pursuing justice, mercy and truth, so, finally, with him, we come to behold the righteousness of God, crucified, raised and glorified.

Amen.

Oliver Gent is a teacher of English and Classics at Bradfield College. He lives in the village with his wife and son. He would like to thank Dr John Cardwell, Mr Roger Keeley, and Mr Stuart Williams for their invaluable assistance.

Published in 2024 by
Unicorn, an imprint of Unicorn Publishing Group
Charleston Studio
Meadow Business Centre
Lewes BN8 5RW
www.unicornpublishing.org

Text copyright © 2024 Oliver Gent

All rights reserved. No part of the contents of this book may be reproduced, stored in or introduced into a retrieval system, or transmitted, in any form or by any means (electronic, mechanical, photocopying, recording or otherwise), without the prior written permission of the copyright holder and the above publisher of this book.

Every effort has been made to trace copyright holders and to obtain their permission for the use of copyrighted material. The publisher apologises for any errors or omissions and would be grateful to be notified of any corrections that should be incorporated in future reprints or editions of this book.

ISBN 978 1 917458 11 5

10 9 8 7 6 5 4 3 2 1

Design by newtonworks.uk

Printed in Latvia by FineTone Ltd

BENEDICTUS ES O DOMINE DOCE ME STATUTA TUA

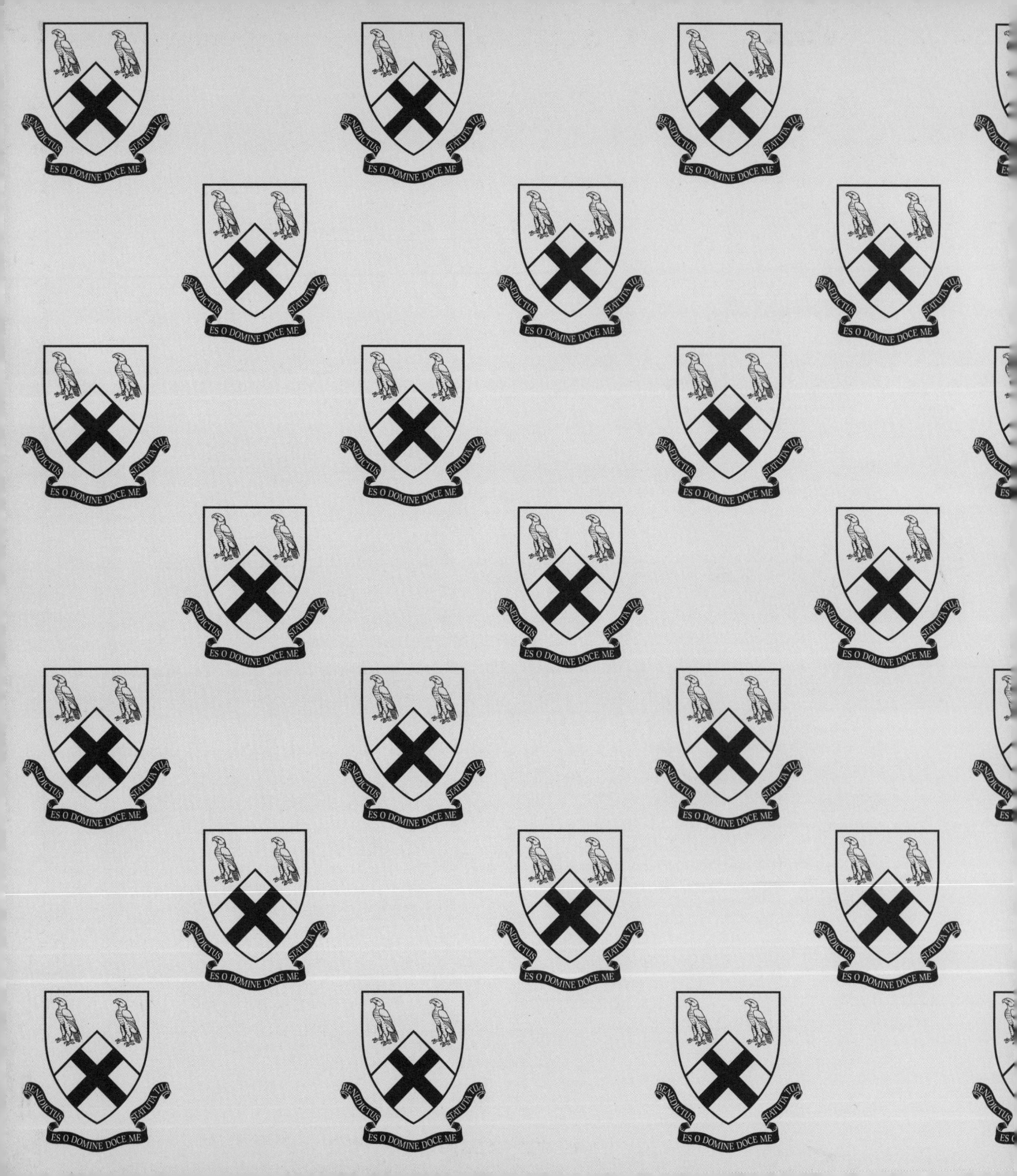